WELSH SPRINGE[R]

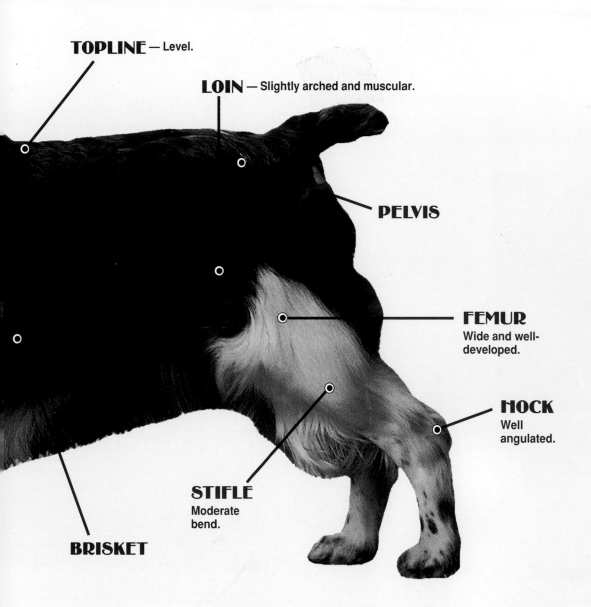

TOPLINE — Level.

LOIN — Slightly arched and muscular.

PELVIS

FEMUR
Wide and well-developed.

HOCK
Well angulated.

STIFLE
Moderate bend.

BRISKET

Title page: Welsh Springer Spaniels owned by Richard and Sandy Rohrbacher.

Photographers: Isabelle Francais, Mary Bloom, Michael and Linda Brennan, Judy Iby, Maggie Rovner, Cindy Sites, Barbara S. Smith, Chuck and Sandy Tatham, Chuck Urland.

© by T.F.H. Publications, Inc.

Distributed in the UNITED STATES to the Pet Trade by T.F.H. Publications, Inc., One T.F.H. Plaza, Neptune City, NJ 07753; distributed in the UNITED STATES to the Bookstore and Library Trade by National Book Network, Inc. 4720 Boston Way, Lanham MD 20706; in CANADA to the Pet Trade by H & L Pet Supplies Inc., 27 Kingston Crescent, Kitchener, Ontario N2B 2T6; Rolf C. Hagen Inc., 3225 Sartelon St. Laurent-Montreal Quebec H4R 1E8; in CANADA to the Book Trade by Vanwell Publishing Ltd., 1 Northrup Crescent, St. Catharines, Ontario L2M 6P5 ; in ENGLAND by T.F.H. Publications, PO Box 15, Waterlooville PO7 6BQ; in AUSTRALIA AND THE SOUTH PACIFIC by T.F.H. (Australia), Pty. Ltd., Box 149, Brookvale 2100 N.S.W., Australia; in NEW ZEALAND by Brooklands Aquarium Ltd. 5 McGiven Drive, New Plymouth, RD1 New Zealand; in Japan by T.F.H. Publications, Japan—Jiro Tsuda, 10-12-3 Ohjidai, Sakura, Chiba 285, Japan; in SOUTH AFRICA by Lopis (Pty) Ltd., P.O. Box 39127, Booysens, 2016, Johannesburg, South Africa. Published by T.F.H. Publications, Inc.

MANUFACTURED IN THE
UNITED STATES OF AMERICA
BY T.F.H. PUBLICATIONS, INC.

WELSH SPRINGER SPANIELS

A COMPLETE AND RELIABLE HANDBOOK

Linda S. Brennan

RX-112

CONTENTS

DESCRIPTION OF THE WELSH SPRINGER SPANIEL

A true sporting dog in temperament, the Welsh Springer Spaniel is a large dog in a mid-sized package. The Welsh is a flushing spaniel—bred to work relatively close to the hunter and to find, flush and retrieve birds and small game both on land and from water. He is also a wonderful pet for the owner who appreciates his unique character.

TEMPERAMENT

The Welsh Springer is a very loyal and devoted family member, and the typical Welsh chooses to spend his time with his family. He is not a one-person dog but is very devoted to the entire family—even extending his loyalties to a circle of friends and other regular visitors. Some Welsh are more reserved with strangers, and in the past there has been a tendency toward shyness in some dogs. However, breeders have been working

The Welsh Springer Spaniel has been bred to work with hunters to find, flush and retrieve game from land and water. This is the breed's first Master Hunter, Briallu Cross Fire, MH, WDX owned by Chuck Urland.

Welsh Springers thrive on family life and get along wonderfully with children. Piper Smith plays with a litter of Briallu puppies.

diligently to improve in this area. Most Welsh do make excellent watch dogs. They are quick to bark at strangers and odd noises and their bark is quite deep and loud for their size.

Most Welsh get along well with other dogs, as well as cats. They are particularly fond of other Welsh Springers. In fact, they often pick out another Welsh at a distance and demand to go and visit. Just like people, though, they are fooled sometimes and the other "Welsh" will turn out to be a Brittany! Of course, problems between dogs can exist, especially between un-neutered males, and caution and training are the best course of action in any multi-dog household. Early socialization helps the young Welsh to be confident and friendly around other dogs. One option is to attend a puppy kindergarten class with your Welshie and allow your young puppy (under six months of age) to interact with other dogs.

Welsh Springers are generally excellent with children but be sure to teach youngsters how to behave around the dog, as well as training the dog to behave around youngsters. A fenced yard is an ideal way for children and dogs to enjoy each other's company and get beneficial exercise in the process. A game of fetch can provide a needed outlet for the dog's energy and entertain the children, while actually reinforcing a very desirable behavior—coming back to the person with an object! Another good way to help reinforce that the dog should obey the children as well as the adults is to allow the child to teach the dog to do some simple tricks. This can be fun for both dog and child and provides a great training opportunity for children who are too young to do formal obedience.

APPEARANCE

The Welsh Springer Spaniel is a medium-sized red and white dog with moderate coat. The average male weighs 45–55 pounds, while the female weighs 35–45 pounds. A male stands 18 to 19 inches, and the female 17 to 18 inches. However, there is considerable variation in size, with some dogs as large as 21 inches or more. The coat is medium in length, with longer feathering on the legs, ears, chest and tail. The tail is customarily docked to about a third of its original length, although undocked Welsh are now seen occasionally since docking has been restricted in some European countries. The color is a rich red—sometimes as dark as the color of an Irish Setter—and white. Some dogs are primarily red on the body, while others are primarily white with patches of red. Characteristically there is a white blaze down the face, with red ears. Legs are generally white,

The Welsh Springer Spaniel is a medium-sized dog donning a rich red and white coat with a characteristic white blaze on the face and freckling on the legs. Fini owned by Caroline Kaplonski.

often with freckling, which is also seen on the muzzle. However, there is no required pattern or preference in markings.

Because Welsh Springers are relatively less known than many of the other spaniel breeds, they are often mistaken for English Springer Spaniels, English Cocker Spaniels, or Cocker Spaniels, as well as Brittanys. The Welsh Springer's color distinguishes him from his English counterparts. The Welsh is always red and white, while the English Springer comes in either black and white or liver (dark brown) and white and can have tan points. The English Springer is also more of a square dog in proportion of length to height, while the Welsh is a

Although actually quite different in appearance, the Welsh Springer is most commonly mistaken for the Brittany, shown here.

rectangle—being slightly longer than tall. The English also has longer ears and more coat. Although Cocker Spaniels and English Cocker Spaniels come in red and white, they are both much smaller and have more coat and longer ears than the Welsh.

The most common mistake made is confusing the Brittany with the Welsh. The Brittany is actually a pointing breed while the Welsh is a flushing spaniel. A well-made Welsh and Brittany are quite different. The Welsh is red while the Brittany is orange, although both colors come in many shades that do seem to overlap at times. The Welsh has dark pigment around the eyes and most have a black or very dark brown nose while the Brittany has liver pigmentation of the eye rims and nose. Also the Brittany is more of a square dog, with proportionately longer legs and lighter bone and has a smaller, higher set ear.

HISTORY OF THE WELSH SPRINGER SPANIEL

Like many breeds, the exact origin of the Welsh Springer is not known with any certainty. As his name suggests, he comes from the British Isles. It has been asserted by some that the Welsh is the oldest of the spaniel breeds and certainly red and white spaniel-type dogs are depicted in works of art dating back several centuries. Red and white spaniels have been

The Welsh Springer is thought to have developed as a flushing spaniel in Wales over four centuries ago. Ch. Briallu Shotgunner Sam, MH, WD owned by Cindy Sites and Chuck Urland.

known to exist in the British Isles for at least four centuries. However, definitive evidence of a red and white spaniel in Wales can only be used to substantiate the breeds existence from the 18th century. The theory exists that the red and white spaniels that seem to have dominated in Britain before the rise of liver or black and whites may have persisted in the remote countryside of Wales.

What is known is that the Welsh Springer is a distinct breed not a variety of the better-known English Springer. In fact, at times there has been talk of

changing the name of the breed to the Welsh Spaniel in order to emphasize the uniqueness of the breed. It is true that they were, in fact, judged together with the English Springer until the breed was officially separated by the Kennel Club of Great Britain in 1902, but Welsh Springers had been shown, up until that time, in a mixed group of spaniels. Once the various spaniel breeds were separated, a club was formed to promote the Welsh Springer. The First World War, however, suspended activity, and the official breed club was not formed until 1924. A steady number of Welsh Springers, between 95 and 139 dogs, were registered with the Kennel Club each year from 1926 to 1938. The numbers then dropped due to World War II. However, they rebounded in 1945 and have continued to grow. The numbers of Welsh competing in the show ring experienced similar trends as well. While still not a common breed even today, the number of Welsh Springers has grown steadily in the country of the breed's origin.

As the breed rebounded after the Second World War, the first post-war British Champion was Dewi Sant, bred by Miss Evans and owned by Harold Newman, in 1947. As of 1990, the all-time record holder for the most wins in breed shows, called Challenge Certificates or CCs, was Sh. Ch. Dalati Sarian, bred and owned by Mr. and Mrs. Hunton Morgans.

The Welsh Springer was officially judged with the English Springer Spaniel, shown here, until they were separated by the Kennel Club of Great Britain in 1902.

HISTORY IN AMERICA

Some sources point to the existence of red and white spaniels in America from the early history on the continent. The American Kennel Club recognized the Welsh Springer in 1906, but did not register the first dog in the breed until 1914. Not much activity existed at that time and, in fact, no Welsh Springers were registered at all by the AKC from 1926 to 1948.

There was a resurgence of activity in the breed in the 1950s, with imports brought in from Britain to provide foundation stock for the breed. Many prominent British kennels have contributed greatly to the gene pool in America and many of the Welsh who have come to the United States are from the top winning kennels in Britain.

There are also active Welsh Springer clubs and fanciers in many other countries. Finland, Sweden, Holland, and other European countries, as well as Australia and Canada, are home to Welsh Springers and their fans. These countries have also contributed to the gene pool of Welsh Springers in America through an exchange of imported and exported dogs, unlike the United Kingdom where the quarantine rule has all but eliminated the import of Welsh Springers from outside Britain. Imported dogs with full undocked tails from some of the Scandinavian countries where tail docking is being eliminated are now competing and winning in American dog shows. The information age is making communication between world-wide Welsh Springer enthusiasts a reality. This global sharing of ideas and information is sure to bring the scattered groups around the world closer together.

Responsible breeding and British importations have saved the Welsh Springer from extinction and contributed to the resurgence of the breed. Kyna owned by Barbara Smith.

STANDARD FOR THE WELSH SPRINGER SPANIEL

For those who fancy the Welsh Springer Spaniel, the standard of the breed is a vital tool in breeding the ideal dog. Inasmuch as the Welsh must perform as a vigorous working dog, the standard describes such a dog, perfect only in that he can do the work for which he was bred.

A standard is a written description of the "ideal dog," a dog that in actuality has never existed and never will. The following standard is the approved standard of the American Kennel Club, the principal governing

A compact dog built for hard work and endurance, the Welsh Springer Spaniel is a dog of distinct variety and ancient origins. Owner, George O'Neill.

body for the dog sport in the United States. The standard is drafted and proposed by the national parent club, and then accepted by AKC. As the parent club sees fit, the standard can change from time to time, though these changes are essentially quite minor, usually pertaining to the format of the standard itself or perhaps some word choice. Studying the breed standard will reveal much about the dog itself, its character, and its ideal physique. Whether you are interested in breeding, showing, or just enjoying your dog, the standard makes required reading for any breed fancier.

The Welsh Springer is primarily a hunting dog, possessing an alert expression. Owners, Cindy Sites and Chuck Urland.

OFFICIAL STANDARD FOR THE WELSH SPRINGER SPANIEL

General Appearance—The Welsh Springer Spaniel is a dog of distinct variety and ancient origin, who derives his name from his hunting style and not his relationship to other breeds. He is an attractive dog of handy size, exhibiting substance without coarseness. He is compact, not leggy, obviously built for hard work and endurance. The Welsh Springer Spaniel gives the impression of length due to obliquely angled forequarters and well developed hindquarters. Being a hunting dog, he should be shown in hard muscled working condition. His coat should not be so excessive as to hinder his work as an active flushing spaniel, but should be thick enough to protect him from heavy cover and weather.

A hardy working spaniel, the Welsh should have a coat that is waterproof and weatherproof. Owner, Caroline Kaplonski.

Size, Proportion, Substance—A dog is ideally 18–19 inches in height at the withers and a bitch is 17–18 inches at the withers. Any animal above or below the ideal to be proportionately penalized. Weight should be in proportion to height and overall balance. Length of body from the withers to the base of the tail is very slightly greater than the distance from the withers to the ground. This body length may be the same as the height but never shorter, thus preserving the rectangular silhouette of the Welsh Springer Spaniel.

Head—The Welsh Springer Spaniel head is unique and should in no way approximate that of other spaniel breeds. Its overall balance is of primary importance.

Head is in proportion to body, never so broad as to appear coarse nor so narrow as to appear racy. The skull is of medium length, slightly domed, with a clearly defined stop. It is well chiseled below the eyes. The top plane of the skull is very slightly divergent from that of the muzzle, but with no tendency toward a down-faced appearance. A short chubby head is most objectionable.

Eyes should be oval in shape, dark to medium brown in color with a soft expression. Preference is for a darker eye though lighter shades of brown are acceptable. Yellow or mean-looking eyes are to be heavily penalized. Medium in size, they are neither prominent, nor sunken, nor do they show haw. Eye rims are tight and dark pigmentation is preferred.

Ears are set on approximately at eye level and hang close to the cheeks. Comparatively small, the leather does not reach to the nose. Gradually narrowing toward the tip, they are shaped somewhat like a vine leaf and are lightly feathered.

The Welsh Springer's head is unique to spaniel breeds, with brown oval eyes and small ears set at eye level. Owner, Sandra Rohrbacher.

The length of the *muzzle* is approximately equal to, but never longer than that of the skull. It is straight, fairly square, and free from excessive flew. Nostrils are well developed and black or any shade of brown in color. A pink nose is to be severely penalized. A scissors *bite* is preferred. An undershot jaw is to be severely penalized.

Neck, Topline, Body—The *neck* is long and slightly arched, clean in throat, and set into long, sloping shoulders.

Topline is level. The loin is slightly arched, muscular, and close-coupled. The croup is very slightly rounded, never steep nor falling off. The topline in combination with proper angulation fore and aft presents a silhouette that appears rectangular. The *chest* is well developed and muscular with a prominent forechest, the ribs well sprung and the brisket reaching to the elbows. The *tail* is an extension of the topline. Carriage is nearly horizontal or slightly elevated when the dog is excited. The tail is generally docked and displays a lively action.

Forequarters—The shoulder blade and upper arm are approximately equal in length. The upper arm is set well back, joining the shoulder blade with sufficient angulation to place the elbow beneath the highest point of the shoulder blade when standing.

The forearms are of medium length, straight and moderately feathered. The legs are well boned but not to the extent of coarseness. The Welsh Springer Spaniel's elbows should be close to the body and its pasterns short and slightly sloping. Height to the elbows is approximately equal to the distance from the elbows to the top of the shoulder blades. Dewclaws are generally removed. Feet should be round, tight and well arched with thick pads.

Hindquarters—The hindquarters must be strong, muscular, and well boned, but not coarse. When viewed in profile the thighs should be wide and the second thighs well developed. The angulation of the pelvis and femur corresponds to that of the shoulder and upper arm. Bend of stifle is moderate. The bones

The Welsh Springer's strong legs allow for his smooth, powerful gait and his tail is usually docked to keep from being injured in the field.

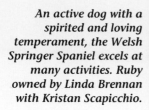

An active dog with a spirited and loving temperament, the Welsh Springer Spaniel excels at many activities. Ruby owned by Linda Brennan with Kristan Scapicchio.

from the hocks to the pads are short with a well angulated hock joint. When viewed from the side or rear they are perpendicular to the ground. Rear dewclaws are removed. Feet as in front.

Coat—The coat is naturally straight flat and soft to the touch, never wiry or wavy. It is sufficiently dense to be waterproof, thornproof, and weatherproof. The back of the forelegs, the hind legs above the hocks, chest and underside of the body are moderately feathered. The ears and tail are lightly feathered. Coat so excessive as to be a hindrance in the field is to be discouraged. Obvious barbering is to be avoided as well.

Color—The color is rich red and white only. Any pattern is acceptable and any white area may be flecked with red ticking.

Gait—The Welsh Springer moves with a smooth, powerful, ground covering action that displays drive from the rear. Viewed from the side, he exhibits a strong forward stride with a reach that does not waste energy. When viewed from the front, the legs should appear to move forward in an effortless manner with no tendency for the feet to cross over or interfere with each other. Viewed from the rear, the hocks should follow on a line with the forelegs, neither too widely nor too closely spaced. As the speed increases the feet tend to converge towards a center line.

Temperament—The Welsh Springer Spaniel is an active dog displaying a loyal and affectionate disposition. Although reserved with strangers, he is not timid, shy nor unfriendly. To this day he remains a devoted family member and hunting companion.

Approved June 13, 1989
Effective August 1, 1989

SHOWING YOUR WELSH SPRINGER SPANIEL

The first Welsh Springer breed champion was Ch. Holiday of Happy Hunting, bred by Mrs. Eleanor P. Howes of East Bridgewater, Massachusetts. "Rush" was born in 1953, and was the product of two imports from the Downland Kennel in Sussex, England. Since then, a growing number of Welsh have completed the requirements for an American championship, starting with a few during the 1950s and 1960s and increasing during the subsequent decades. In 1996, 41 Welsh Springers became champions.

UCD Ch. Briallu Ruby Tuesday, UD, Can. CDX, WD, VC, owned by Linda Brennan, is a fine example of the versatile Welsh Springer Spaniel.

The Welsh Springer Spaniel Club of America (WSSCA) was started in 1961 by a small group of about 20 families of active Welsh owners. In 1980, the club held its first National Specialty show in conjunction with the Penn Treaty Kennel Club in Pennsylvania. The Best of Breed winner at the first specialty, Ch. Randail Taffy of Sylabru, bred by Sylvia Foreacre and owned by H.R. Randolph, went on to win again in 1984. The national special continued to be held in Pennsylvania until 1990, when the show was held in Ohio. Since then, the national specialty has been rotated to different areas of the country each year, allowing Welsh Springer fanciers from around the country an opportunity to see the biggest show of the

Ch. Rysan's First Round Kayo, CDX winning Best of Breed at the Welsh Springer Spaniel Club of America National Specialty. Owners, Richard and Sandy Rohrbacher.

year in the breed. Entries at local shows are generally small, with shows in many locations lacking any Welsh Springer entries, but the National Specialty shows typically bring together a hundred or more Welsh at a time! Regional specialties, in addition to the annual National Specialty, are also held occasionally and the first was held in Kentucky in 1987. These events also help to provide opportunities for Welsh and their people to get together to interact and celebrate their common love of the breed.

Another important show for Welsh Springer exhibitors is the annual American Spaniel Club all-flushing spaniel show held each January in New Jersey. This

show is another opportunity for a relatively large number of Welsh, sometimes 50 or more, to gather. This prestigious and competitive show is open to all of the flushing spaniel breeds only. In 1985, a Welsh Springer, Ch. Fracas Little Caeser, owned and bred by Frances Bloom, became the first and only Welsh Springer to win Best in Show there. "Little C" also had an all-breed BIS, which is a rarity in this breed. Although Welsh Springers are becoming more competitive in the demanding world of high-level conformation competition, there have been only a few to achieve top honors. Ch. Rysan's First Round Kayo, CDX, bred by Sandra and Richard Rohrbacher, became a multiple all-breed BIS winner with two top honors in the early 1990s.

WSSCA also gives annual awards to the top Welsh in conformation showing (the Deckard's Cup) and the top female Welsh (the Olympian Trophy) owned by a member of the club. Awards are also given in obedience (the Ch. Cicero Gus UDT Cup) and for the top owner-handled Welsh in conformation. Another program, instituted in 1990, is the versatility program. The Club recognizes Welsh Springers who are accomplished in all areas — breed showing, obedience competition, and the hunting field — with the titles VC

Kelsey, owned by Linda Brennan, is practicing for the obedience ring. Kelsey has earned her American and Canadian CDX.

(Versatility Certificate) and VCX (Versatility Certificate Excellent). This program provides important recognition for those dogs who excel in all areas and, thus, encourages the breeding of well-rounded dogs who can compete in the show ring and still retain the instinct and trainability to perform the breeds original purpose—working as a flushing spaniel.

There are also regional Welsh Springer clubs in parts of the United States. Although the Welsh is not a very common breed, there are a few areas of the country that do a have a relatively large concentration of Welsh Springers. Local clubs have formed in these areas and serve to provide local contacts, information and activities to area fanciers. The main areas supported by local clubs are: the Northeast in the New

Although they are not commonly seen in the Junior Showmanship ring, a well-trained Welsh makes an excellent partner for the junior handler. Ruby with Kristan Scapicchio.

Jersey area, the Mid-Atlantic in the Virginia area, the South in the Georgia area, the Mid-West in the Wisconsin area, and the Southwest around Arizona and Southern California areas. Local breeders and the WSSCA can provide information on local clubs.

OBEDIENCE COMPETITION

Although the Welsh Springer is not a popular choice for obedience, there have been a record of successful Welsh competitors. In the AKC system of obedience, there are three levels of competition: Novice, Open, and Utility. These tests result in the titles: Companion Dog (CD), Companion Dog Excellent (CDX), and Utility Dog (UD), respectively. Beyond these titles, after additional competition the dogs can earn the Utility Dog Excellent (UDX) and Obedience Trial Champion (OTCH) titles.

SHOWING

The first Welsh Springer earned an obedience title, CD, in 1956. The first Welsh to complete a Utility Dog title was Ch. Cicero Gus, UDT, owned by Mr. and Mrs. Charles Hatz and bred by Stanley Spirala, in 1971. To date, ten Welsh Springers have earned a UD. It is interesting to note that a majority, seven out of ten, are also breed champions. In 1995 and 1996, breed history was made when the first UDX and the first OTCH were both earned by OTCH. Glyndwir Fwyn Celsey, UDX, owned by Cathy Soule and bred by Janet Ing. The number or Welsh Springers competing in obedience is not large but there is a steady following. Those dedicated to obedience are very support-

Many Welsh Springer Spaniels love the water and are natural retrievers. Cindy Sites with Sam and Bozwell, two Master Hunters.

ive of each other, and the new Welsh owner who is interested in obedience should seek out those in the breed who are willing to share their experiences.

There are other outlets for the energetic Welsh Springer as well. The newly popular sport of agility is one to which the Welsh is well-suited. The athletic and trainable Welsh, with a hint of independence, usually loves to perform on the agility course. After basic obedience training, agility is an excellent option for the Welsh Springer and owner who want to continue to participate in organized dog sports.

24

HUNTING TITLES

Until the AKC started their hunting test program, the only available field competitions for Welsh Springers were those offered by WSSCA. These include the WD/WDX program and informal field trials. The WD/WDX program consists of a non-competitive test of the dogs ability to find, flush, and retrieve birds on land and retrieve birds from water. The dog need pass the test only once to be awarded the title. The WD, "Working Dog" title is given to the dog who passes each part of the test; the WDX, "Working Dog Excellent" title is give to the dog who is rated excellent in each area of the test. Thus, it is the same test for both titles, and it is the dog's proficiency that determines which title is awarded. The test is a good indication of basic hunting instinct, including retrieving, and some beginning level of training, mostly the ability to control the dog in the field. Numerous WD and WDX titles have been awarded by WSSCA through the years. Some of these dogs have gone on to participate in AKC hunting tests.

Around 1988, the AKC expanded its new Hunting Test program to include flushing spaniels. The tests sanctioned by the AKC include three distinct levels, each with a different test and resulting title. The tests are non-competitive and the dog must pass the test at a particular level a set number of times in order to receive the title. The Junior Hunter, JH, title requires that the dog pass the Junior level test four times, while the Senior Hunter, SH, requires five passes at the Senior level and the Master Hunter, MH, requires six passes at the Master level. A dog need not earn the JH before the SH, or the SH before the MH. However, a dog is given credit for one SH pass if it has already earned a JH title, and one MH pass if it has the SH title.

In the field, the Welsh Springer exhibits innate hunting abilities combined with instinctual judgment and skill. Owner, Linda Brennan.

The majority of Welsh Springers with hunting titles are also breed champions, proving that form has been bred with function. Truepenny's Lady Cyfeillgar, UD, WD owned by Shirlee O'Neill.

The Junior Hunter test is similar to the WD test in what is required of the dog. The Senior test requires that the dog be trained to a higher level, be under better control, and do a "hunt dead" where the dog does not see the bird fall and must use direction from the handler and its nose to find the bird. The Master level requires a fully polished hunting dog. The dog must be "steady to wing and shot," in other words, the dog must freeze into a sit after flushing the bird and while the gunner shoots the bird, then, when directed by the handler, the dog retrieves the bird. This level of training is truly impressive to watch.

The AKC awarded the first hunting titles to Welsh Springers in 1989 with Briallu Cross Fire, WDX ("Bozwell") owned by Chuck Urland and bred by Barbara Smith, and Ch. Wynfomeer's Lu-C Nor'Easter, CD, WDX, VCX ("Dfydd"), owned by Wynfomeer Kennels, handled by Ned Cummings, and bred by Sheila Hiles, completed the first JH titles on the same day. To date, there have been three Master Hunter Welsh. "Bozwell" went on to earn the first Master Hunter title. The second, and first breed champion, was his housemate Ch. Briallu Shotgunners Sam, WD, MH, owned by Cindy Sites and Chuck Urland and bred by Barbara and Richard Smith. "Dfydd" became the third Master Hunter. The most impressive thing about examining the list of Welsh Springers with hunting titles is that the majority are also breed champions. This is very encouraging, in that it indicates that the competitive Welsh Springer retains its hunting instincts. In other words, form is following function.

THE WELSH SPRINGER SPANIEL AS A PET

The Welsh Springer is a hardy active hunting dog and a loyal family pet. He does best when kept in the house — his natural desire to be a part of the family will result in a loud display of displeasure if he is kept primarily outdoors. The typical Welsh Springer follows his person around the house and will even camp outside the bathroom door while his owner showers. He is always happiest in the company of his family.

Welsh are happiest when in the company of their family. Ch. Sylabru's Red, White And True, Ch. Truepenny's Dewi M'Dad and Ch. Truepenny Talisman owned by Marion Daniel pose for a family portrait.

The Welsh is not the right breed for someone who is looking for a dog to have around only when he or she feels like interacting with him and then ignore him the rest of the time. Welsh Springers are not pushy in demanding constant attention from their owners; however, they are happiest in their owners' presence. With enough exercise, a Welsh will happily curl up at your feet all evening as you watch television but will protest loudly if he were locked in the garage or basement. Crate training, which is the best course of action for virtually all dogs, will produce a Welsh Springer who can confidently be left alone; but when you are in the house, he will want to be with you.

As an active dog bred for hunting, the Welsh Springer requires daily exercise. A long walk or energetic romp in the fenced-in yard with the kids is a necessity each day. A vigorous game of fetch with a tennis ball in an enclosed area is an excellent way to exercise your dog after a tough day at the office. A healthy outlet for the dog's natural energy will prevent many undesirable behaviors, such as barking, chewing, digging and other destructive behavior.

Early obedience training is an excellent recommendation for the Welsh Springer puppy. Although Welsh were developed to work with people as hunting companions, they can have an independent streak. The time to train the young dog is as early as possible and also be sure to provide opportunities to socialize the puppy with other people and animals. Because some Welsh can be a bit timid around strangers or new situations, it is best to provide them with lots of positive experiences while they are young. Approach training with a positive attitude and your Welsh Springer will respond well. Find a training school or trainer who knows how to use positive reinforcement to make

A hardy working dog, the Welsh Springer Spaniel thrives in any kind of climate. Mazie, Wynonah and Briallen owned by Barbara and Richard Smith.

An active dog bred for the outdoor life, the Welsh Springer requires daily exercise as an outlet for his natural energy.

training a pleasurable experience for both you and your puppy. Training should also include corrections when necessary to reinforce behavior once the dog understands what is expected and simply chooses not to obey. A balanced approach to training is best for most dogs, Welsh Springers included.

HUNTING ABILITY

As indicated previously, the Welsh Springer Spaniel is a flushing spaniel. His job throughout history has been to find, flush, and retrieve game, including waterfowl, upland game birds, and small game, such as rabbits. His name comes from the characteristic spaniel function of flushing or "springing" game. In style, he is a steady and tireless worker, not as fast and flashy as the English Springer nor as slow and methodical as some of the heavier slower spaniels.

One excellent feature of the breed is the fact that most dogs still retain their hunting instincts. Many breeds, especially the more popular ones, evolve into distinct lines, some excelling in the hunting field,

29

Your Welsh puppy should begin obedience training early and learn to work with and trust his owner.

others in the show ring and still others in the obedience ring. Welsh Springers have not yet, and one hopes never will, suffer this fate. When looking for a likely hunting prospect, one would do best to purchase a dog bred from dogs that are known still to possess the required drive and instinct. This can be demonstrated by a dog who is used as an actual hunting companion or by dogs who have earned titles in the hunting field. Although Welsh Springers, due to their rarity, are not allowed in licensed field trials in the United States, which are reserved for English Springers and Cocker Spaniels, there are two excellent outlets for field testing available. One is the American Kennel Club's Hunting Test Program, where dogs compete in a pass-fail test at three different levels: Junior, Senior and Master. The other is the Welsh Springer Spaniel Club of America's Working Dog/ Working Dog Excellent program. This is a somewhat less formal test, but still indicative of instinct and some level of trainability. The WD/WDX test must be passed only once to earn the title, while the AKC's JH, SH, and MH titles require four, five and six passes respectively.

As a prospective hunting companion, the Welsh Springer puppy should be started with basic obedience early. Although, as a sporting dog, the Welsh Springer is very trainable, he can be a bit independent, particularly in the field. If not taught to work with his owner, he may decide to go on a grand romp in the field or have fun chasing game in a very unproductive manner. Many Welsh Springers are natural retrievers, but some do not have the softest of mouths and some basic retrieving training is in order.

Many Welsh Springers love to swim. Although some Welsh are reluctant to enter water, many enjoy the chance to swim and retrieve. Rarely do Welsh have the dramatic water entry of the Labrador Retriever or some English Springers, but there are some who can even compete on this level. Again, starting with your puppy early and letting him have exposure and positive experiences in life is the best plan. Taking a puppy along with other grown dogs who like to swim and retrieve from water is often an easy way of getting the pup to venture out. Otherwise, it may be necessary for the owner to get into the water to encourage the puppy to come in.

An excellent way to get started in field training is to find a group of enthusiastic hunters near you. Through contacts in the various clubs, one can find those who are active in their area. Another option is to attend hunting test and working dog tests. This provides an

If you introduce your Welsh to the water slowly at a young age, he should have no trouble learning to retrieve. Here Samantha, owned by Barbara and Richard Smith, is participating in a working test.

opportunity to see the dogs in action, as well as meet their owners. Because many breeders are interested in preserving the ability of Welsh and continuing to promote their traditional functions, they are also a good reference for training. If they don't participate in field training and activities personally, they can usually direct you to others who do so locally. It is best to find someone to work with and advise you who has experience with Welsh Springers specifically, although this is not always possible.

GROOMING YOUR WELSH SPRINGER SPANIEL

The Welsh Springer is a breed that does require regular grooming. The self-cleaning coat makes bathing an infrequent necessity, but an occasional bath is in order if the dog gets particularly dirty or picks up a foul odor, for example after a swim in a murky pond. Regular brushing, preferably daily, is a quick and easy way to maintain the coat. A proper Welsh coat does not mat easily, but the softer undercoat and feathering, especially under the elbows and on the rear legs, can develop mats if tangles and burrs are not quickly attended. A daily brushing also gives the

The Welsh Springer Spaniel is a breed that requires regular grooming, and daily brushing is a great way to maintain his coat and keep it free of mats.

owner a chance to go over the dog quickly on a regular basis, thus calling attention to any minor cuts, wounds, or other problems.

The trimming necessary for the well-groomed pet is minimal and certainly within the ability of most owners. The ears should be trimmed, particularly on the underside of the ear leather. Clippers or scissors should be used to remove all excess hair on the underside of the ear flap. This allows a constant flow of air into the ear canal. Trimming, combined with occasional ear cleaning, eliminates virtually all ear problems, which spaniels are prone to with their long and heavy ears. To clean the ear, use a commercial

Spaniels are prone to ear problems because of their long and heavy ears, so be sure to trim the hair on the flap and clean the ear canal regularly. Owners, Richard and Sandy Rohrbacher.

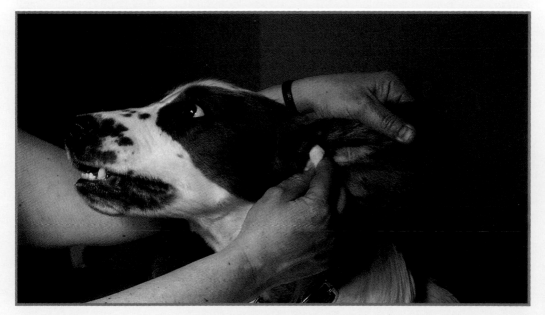

ear cleaning solution on a cotton ball once every few weeks. It is also a good idea to clean the dog's ears after a swim to remove any water that may be trapped in the ear. If you notice the dog scratching at his ears or rubbing them against the carpet or furniture, check to see if any redness or swelling are present in the ear canal. If the redness persists after a thorough cleaning, an ear infection may be present and a trip to the veterinarian is necessary.

The other area on the Welsh Springer that needs attention is the feet. The Welsh Springer, like many other dogs bred to retrieve from water, has a webbed foot. If the dog is born with any dewclaws (the fifth toe, which is above the foot) on the front or rear legs, they should be removed by the breeder. This should be done at the same time the tail is docked, when the

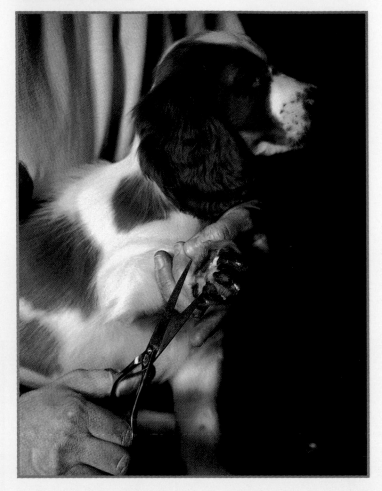

It is best to trim the hair around your Welsh Springer's feet. This allows them better footing and keeps the tracking of dirt and mud into your house to a minimum.

puppies are two or three days old. The nails should be kept short with frequent trimming. Start when the dog is a young puppy; ideally his breeder has started trimming his nails before sending the puppy to his new home. Use a guillotine-type clipper and remove just a tiny tip of the nail at a time. Do the nails once a week when the dog is a puppy and approximately twice a month once the dog is an adult. By trimming nails frequently, you need only cut a small tip off of each nail, thus minimizing the risk of hitting the "quick," or the tiny vain in the nail, and causing it to bleed. Frequent nail trimming will also get the dog accustomed to the procedure and, if you never cause the dog any pain, he will not regard it as unpleasant. A few treats fed to the dog while cutting nails will help the dog to have a better attitude about the procedure.

It is best to trim the hair on the feet also. As mentioned previously, the dog without big hairy "slippers" of fur will track in much less mud and dirt, as well has have better footing and be less likely to slip on smooth floors. Use short grooming shears to trim the hair around the sides of the feet to the edge of the foot. Trim the hair that protrudes on the bottom of the foot between the pads even with the pads. Do not trim the hair between the pads up between the toes, or the dog's foot will splay—the toes will separate and flatten the foot.

Finally, if the tail is docked, the hair on the tail should be trimmed to just beyond the length of the tail. However, some owners enjoy letting the dog have a "flag" of hair at the end of the tail.

For the pet Welsh, the routine grooming can be handled by the owner, without need of a professional grooming. If you choose to go the route of the grooming shop, most groomers will treat the Welsh the same as the English Springer. There are some important differences that you should point out before letting them get to work on your Welshie. The Welsh has a

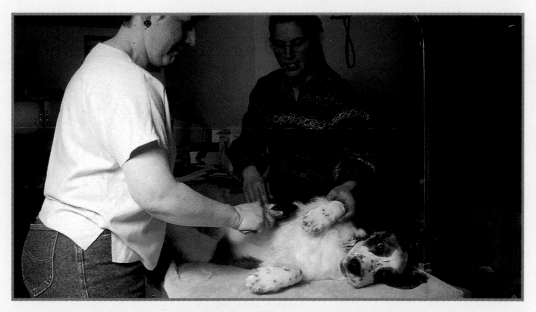

A Welsh Springer Spaniel's coat should never be clipped. Regular brushing is all that is needed to retain the coat's utility and attractiveness.

shorter ear, and the hair on the ear should be trimmed to the shape of the ear leather, rather than letting the hair grow long to provide the look of a longer ear. Most importantly, the body coat of the Welsh Springer should not be clipped. Due to the Welsh Springer's silkier, oilier coat, there is no need to use clippers on the coat. That will, in fact, destroy the self-cleaning property and attractive nature of the coat. Regular brushing is all that is needed to prevent knots and mats from forming in the undercoat.

For the show ring, somewhat more grooming is required than for the pet Welsh, but the breed is not meant to be overly coated or excessively sculpted. In addition to neatening the ears, tail, and feet, the show dog generally has the whiskers, head, neck, and feathering trimmed as well. The head is groomed to remove any stray or fuzzy hair, often using a stripping stone or knife. The head should not be shaved, with the exception of the ears, which may be clipped or thinned using thinning shears. Generally, the whiskers are trimmed to neaten the appearance of the muzzle, but this is not required. The ears are trimmed with the clippers or thinning shears to blend the top of the ear into the skull, as well as to remove excess hair under the ear so that the ear hangs freely against the head. The hair is then trimmed to just beyond the ear leather to follow the vine-leaf shape of the ear.

The neck is generally clipped or thinned to create a smooth look above the breast bone, with the ruff of hair beginning there. The feathering on the legs is trimmed to remove flyaways and neaten the overall appearance. The feet and tail are groomed to remove excess hair. Finally, the dog is brushed until the glossy red and white coat shines. The final product should be a dog who looks neat and catches the eye but who still looks like he could withstand a day of hunting in close cover and swimming. The head, as one of the distinctive features of the breed, should be groomed to accentuate its beauty.

Grooming for the show ring is a more involved process, but the Welsh Springer Spaniel is not meant to be presented as overly sculpted or heavily groomed.

YOUR PUPPY'S NEW HOME

Before actually collecting your puppy, it is better that you purchase the basic items you will need in advance of the pup's arrival date. This allows you more opportunity to shop around and ensure you have exactly what you want rather than having to buy lesser quality in a hurry.

It is always better to collect the puppy as early in the day as possible. In most instances this will mean that

Caring for a puppy is a serious responsibility, so be sure both your household and your family are prepared for your pup's arrival. Aled owned by Marion Daniel and Maggie Rovner.

the puppy has a few hours with your family before it is time to retire for his first night's sleep away from his former home.

If the breeder is local, then you may not need any form of box to place the puppy in when you bring him home. A member of the family can hold the pup in his lap—duly protected by some towels just in case the puppy becomes car sick! Be sure to advise the

Make sure your home is equipped with a safe and secure fenced-in yard for your puppy to go exploring in. Owners, Richard and Sandy Rohrbacher.

breeder at what time you hope to arrive for the puppy, as this will obviously influence the feeding of the pup that morning or afternoon. If you arrive early in the day, then they will likely only give the pup a light breakfast so as to reduce the risk of travel sickness.

If the trip will be of a few hours duration, you should take a travel crate with you. The crate will provide your pup with a safe place to lie down and rest during the trip. During the trip, the puppy will no doubt wish to relieve his bowels, so you will have to make a few stops. On a long journey you may need a rest yourself, and can take the opportunity to let the puppy get some fresh air. However, do not let the puppy walk where there may have been a lot of other dogs because he might pick up an infection. Also, if he relieves his bowels at such a time, do not just leave the feces where they were dropped. This is the height of irresponsibility. It has resulted in many public parks and other places actually banning dogs. You can purchase poop-scoops from your pet shop and should have them with you whenever you are taking the dog out where he might foul a public place.

Your journey home should be made as quickly as possible. If it is a hot day, be sure the car interior is amply supplied with fresh air. It should never be too hot or too cold for the puppy. The pup must never be placed where he might be subject to a draft. If the journey requires an overnight stop at a motel, be aware that other guests will not appreciate a puppy crying half the night. You must regard the puppy as a baby and comfort him so he does not cry for long periods. The worst thing you can do is to shout at or smack him. This will mean your relationship is off to a really bad start. You wouldn't smack a baby, and your puppy is still very much just this.

ON ARRIVING HOME

By the time you arrive home the puppy may be very tired, in which case he should be taken to his sleeping area and allowed to rest. Children should not be allowed to interfere with the pup when he is sleeping. If the pup is not tired, he can be allowed to investigate his new home—but always under your close supervision. After a short look around,

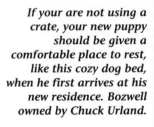

If your are not using a crate, your new puppy should be given a comfortable place to rest, like this cozy dog bed, when he first arrives at his new residence. Bozwell owned by Chuck Urland.

the puppy will no doubt appreciate a light meal and a drink of water. Do not overfeed him at his first meal because he will be in an excited state and more likely to be sick.

Although it is an obvious temptation, you should not invite friends and neighbors around to see the new arrival until he has had at least 48 hours in which to settle down. Indeed, if you can delay this longer then do so, especially if the puppy is not fully vaccinated. At the very least, the visitors might introduce some local bacteria on their clothing that the puppy is not immune to. This aspect is always a risk when a pup has been moved some distance, so the fewer people the pup meets in the first week or so the better.

DANGERS IN THE HOME

Your home holds many potential dangers for a little mischievous puppy, so you must think about these in advance and be sure he is protected from them. The more obvious are as follows:

Open Fires. All open fires should be protected by a mesh screen guard so there is no danger of the pup being burned by spitting pieces of coal or wood.

Electrical Wires. Puppies just love chewing on things, so be sure that all electrical appliances are neatly hidden from view and are not left plugged in when not in use. It is not sufficient simply to turn the plug switch to the off position—pull the plug from the socket.

Keep your Welsh puppies busy and out of trouble by giving them plenty of Gumabones® and Nylafloss® to chew on.

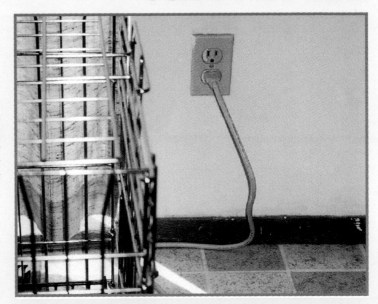

Puppies love to chew on things so make sure all electrical appliances are neatly hidden from view and unplugged when not in use.

Open Doors. A door would seem a pretty innocuous object, yet with a strong draft it could kill or injure a puppy easily if it is slammed shut. Always ensure there is no risk of this happening. It is most likely during warm weather when you have windows or outside doors open and a sudden gust of wind blows through.

Balconies. If you live in a high-rise building, obviously the pup must be protected from falling. Be sure he cannot get through any railings on your patio, balcony, or deck.

Ponds and Pools. A garden pond or a swimming pool is a very dangerous place for a little puppy to be near. Be sure it is well screened so there is no risk of the pup falling in. It takes barely a minute for a pup—or a child—to drown.

The Kitchen. While many puppies will be kept in the kitchen, at least while they are toddlers and not able to control their bowel movements, this is a room full of danger—especially while you are cooking. When cooking, keep the puppy in a play pen or in another room where he is safely out of harm's way. Alternatively, if you have a carry box or crate, put him in this so he can still see you but is well protected.

Be aware, when using washing machines, that more than one puppy has clambered in and decided to have a nap and received a wash instead! If you leave the washing machine door open and leave the room for any reason, then be sure to check inside the machine before you close the door and switch on.

Small Children. Toddlers and small children should never be left unsupervised with puppies. In spite of such advice it is amazing just how many people not only do this but also allow children to pull and maul pups. They should be taught from the outset that a puppy is not a plaything to be dragged about the home—and they should be promptly scolded if they disobey.

Children must be shown how to lift a puppy so it is safe. Failure by you to correctly educate your children about dogs could one day result in their getting a very nasty bite or scratch. When a puppy is lifted, his weight must always be supported. To lift the pup, first place your right hand under his chest. Next, secure

Owning a Welsh Springer puppy is a lifelong commitment guaranteed to bring you a basketful of joy and happiness! Truepenny Barnstormer owned by Maggie Rovner.

the pup by using your left hand to hold his neck. Now you can lift him and bring him close to your chest. Never lift a pup by his ears and, while he can be lifted by the scruff of his neck where the fur is loose, there is no reason ever to do this, so don't.

Beyond the dangers already cited you may be able to think of other ones that are specific to your home— steep basement steps or the like. Go around your home and check out all potential problems—you'll be glad you did.

THE FIRST NIGHT

The first few nights a puppy spends away from his mother and littermates are quite traumatic for him. He will feel very lonely, maybe cold, and will certainly miss the heartbeat of his siblings when sleeping. To help overcome his loneliness it may help to place a clock next to his bed—one with a loud tick. This will in some way soothe him, as the clock ticks to a rhythm not dissimilar from a heart beat. A cuddly toy may also help in the first few weeks. A dim nightlight may provide some comfort to the puppy, because his eyes will not yet be fully able to see in the dark. The puppy may want to leave his bed for a drink or to relieve himself.

If the pup does whimper in the night, there are two things you should not do. One is to get up and chastise him, because he will not understand why you are shouting at him; and the other is to rush to comfort him every time he cries because he will quickly realize that if he wants you to come running all he needs to do is to holler loud enough!

By all means give your puppy some extra attention on his first night, but after this quickly refrain from so doing. The pup will cry for a while but then settle down and go to sleep. Some pups are, of course, worse than others in this respect, so you must use balanced judgment in the matter. Many owners take their pups to bed with them, and there is certainly nothing wrong with this.

The pup will be no trouble in such cases. However, you should only do this if you intend to let this be a permanent arrangement, otherwise it is hardly fair to the puppy. If you have decided to have two puppies, then they will keep each other company and you will have few problems.

It may be tempting to show off your new puppy, but make sure your Welsh Springer has had his proper vaccinations before introducing him to strangers or other pets.

OTHER PETS

If you have other pets in the home then the puppy must be introduced to them under careful supervision. Puppies will get on just fine with any other pets—but you must make due allowance for the respective sizes of the pets concerned, and appreciate that your puppy has a rather playful nature. It would be very foolish to leave him with a young rabbit. The pup will want to play and might bite the bunny and get altogether too rough with it. Kittens are more able to defend themselves from overly cheeky pups, who will get a quick scratch if they overstep the mark. The adult cat could obviously give the pup a very bad scratch, though generally cats will jump clear of pups and watch them from a suitable vantage point. Eventually they will meet at ground level where the cat will quickly hiss and box a puppy's ears. The pup will soon learn to respect an adult cat; thereafter they will probably develop into great friends as the pup matures into an adult dog.

Opposite: Once your puppy leaves for his new home, he will miss the company of his littermates. Give him extra attention during this lonely time.

HOUSETRAINING

Undoubtedly, the first form of training your puppy will undergo is in respect to his toilet habits. To achieve this you can use either newspaper, or a large litter tray filled with soil or lined with newspaper. A puppy cannot control his bowels until he is a few months old, and not fully until he is an adult. Therefore you must anticipate his needs and be prepared for a few accidents. The prime times a pup will urinate and defecate are shortly after he wakes up from a sleep, shortly after he has eaten, and after he has been playing awhile. He will usually whimper and start searching the room for a suitable place. You must quickly pick him up and place him on the newspaper or in the litter tray. Hold him in position gently but firmly. He might jump out of the box without doing anything on the first one or two occasions, but if you simply repeat the procedure every time you think he wants to relieve himself then eventually he will get the message.

When he does defecate as required, give him plenty of praise, telling him what a good puppy he is. The litter tray or newspaper must, of course, be cleaned or replaced after each use—puppies do not like using a dirty toilet any more than you do. The pup's toilet can be placed near the kitchen door and as he gets older the tray can be placed outside while the door is open. The pup will then start to use it while he is outside. From that time on, it is easy to get the pup to use a given area of the yard.

Many breeders recommend the popular alternative of crate training. Upon bringing the pup home, introduce him to his crate. The open wire crate is the best choice, placed in a restricted, draft-free area of the home. Put the pup's Nylabone® and other favorite toys in the crate along with a wool blanket or other suitable bedding. The puppy's natural cleanliness instincts prohibit him from soiling in the place where he sleeps, his crate. The puppy should be allowed to go in and out of the open crate during the day, but he should sleep in the crate at the night and at other intervals during the day. Whenever the pup is taken out of his crate, he should be brought outside (or to his newspapers) to do his business. Never use the crate as a place of punishment. You will see how quickly your pup takes to his crate, considering it as his own safe haven from the big world around him.

THE EARLY DAYS

You will no doubt be given much advice on how to bring up your puppy. This will come from dog-owning friends, neighbors, and through articles and books

When housetraining your puppy on paper, take him to the same spot every time and gradually move the paper close to the door. Owners, Richard and Sandy Rohrbacher.

The Welsh Springer Spaniel will have no trouble getting along with other pets as long as they are properly introduced.

you may read on the subject. Some of the advice will be sound, some will be nothing short of rubbish. What you should do above all else is to keep an open mind and let common sense prevail over prejudice and worn-out ideas that have been handed down over the centuries. There is no one way that is superior to all others, no more than there is no one dog that is exactly a replica of another. Each is an individual and must always be regarded as such.

A dog never becomes disobedient, unruly, or a menace to society without the full consent of his owner. Your puppy may have many limitations, but the singular biggest limitation he is confronted with in so many instances is his owner's inability to understand his needs and how to cope with them.

IDENTIFICATION

It is a sad reflection on our society that the number of dogs and cats stolen every year runs into many thousands. To these can be added the number that get lost. If you do not want your cherished pet to be lost or stolen, then you should see that he is carrying a permanent identification number, as well as a temporary tag on his collar.

Permanent markings come in the form of tattoos placed either inside the pup's ear flap, or on the inner side of a pup's upper rear leg. The number given is then recorded with one of the national registration companies. Research laboratories will not purchase dogs carrying numbers as they realize these are clearly someone's pet, and not abandoned animals. As a result, thieves will normally abandon dogs so marked and this at least gives the dog a chance to be taken to the police or the dog pound, when the number can be traced and the dog reunited with its family. The only problem with this method at this time is that there are a number of registration bodies, so it is not always apparent which one the dog is registered with (as you

Opposite: Due to their softer composition, Gumabones® are perfect for teething puppies.

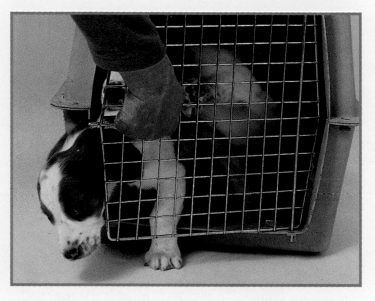

Crate training is a great way to housebreak your Welsh puppy because dogs do not like to soil where they eat and sleep. Owners, Richard and Sandy Rohrbacher.

provide the actual number). However, each registration body is aware of his competitors and will normally be happy to supply their addresses. Those holding the dog can check out which one you are with. It is not a perfect system, but until such is developed it's the best available.

A temporary tag takes the form of a metal or plastic disk large enough for you to place the dog's name and your phone number on it—maybe even your address as well. In virtually all places you will be required to obtain a license for your puppy. This may not become applicable until the pup is six months old, but it might apply regardless of his age. Much depends upon the state within a country, or the country itself, so check with your veterinarian if the breeder has not already advised you on this.

FEEDING YOUR WELSH SPRINGER SPANIEL

Dog owners today are fortunate in that they live in an age when considerable cash has been invested in the study of canine nutritional requirements. This means dog food manufacturers are very concerned about ensuring that their foods are of the best quality. The result of all of their studies, apart from the food itself, is that dog owners are bombarded with advertisements telling them why they must pur-

Your Welsh puppy will receive his first nutrients from his mother, but the breeder should have him eating a commercial diet by the time you are ready to take him home.

chase a given brand. The number of products available to you is unlimited, so it is hardly surprising to find that dogs in general suffer from obesity and an excess of vitamins, rather than the reverse. Be sure to feed age-appropriate food—puppy food up to one year of age, adult food thereafter. Generally breeders recommend dry food supplemented by canned, if needed.

Puppies need well-balanced meals to provide them with the energy they need for proper growth. Owners, Richard and Sandy Rohrbacher.

FACTORS AFFECTING NUTRITIONAL NEEDS

Activity Level. A dog that lives in a country environment and is able to exercise for long periods of the day will need more food than the same breed of dog living in an apartment and given little exercise.

Quality of the Food. Obviously the quality of food will affect the quantity required by a puppy. If the nutritional content of a food is low then the puppy will need more of it than if a better quality food was fed.

Balance of Nutrients and Vitamins. Feeding a puppy the correct balance of nutrients is not easy because the average person is not able to measure out ratios of one to another, so it is a case of trying to see that nothing is in excess. However, only tests, or your veterinarian, can be the source of reliable advice.

Genetic and Biological Variation. Apart from all of the other considerations, it should be remembered that each puppy is an individual. His genetic make-up will influence not only his physical characteristics but also his metabolic efficiency. This being so, two pups from the same litter can vary quite a bit in the amount of food they need to perform the same function under the same conditions. If you consider the potential combinations of all of these factors then you will see that pups of a given breed could vary quite a bit in the amount of food they will need. Before discussing feeding quantities it is valuable to know at least a little about the composition of food and its role in the body.

COMPOSITION AND ROLE OF FOOD

The main ingredients of food are protein, fats, and carbohydrates, each of which is needed in relatively large quantities when compared to the other needs of vitamins and minerals. The other vital ingredient of food is, of course, water. Although all foods obviously contain some of the basic ingredients needed for an animal to survive, they do not all contain the ingredients in the needed ratios or type. For example, there are many forms of protein, just as there are many types of carbohydrates. Both of these compounds are found in meat and in vegetable matter—but not all of those that are needed will be in one particular meat or vegetable. Plants, especially, do not contain certain amino acids that are required for the synthesis of certain proteins needed by dogs.

Likewise, vitamins are found in meats and vegetable matter, but vegetables are a richer source of most. Meat contains very little carbohydrates. Some vitamins can be synthesized by the dog, so do not

POPpups™ are 100% edible and enhanced with dog friendly ingredients like liver, cheese, spinach, carrots or potatoes. They contain no salt, sugar, alcohol, plastic or preservatives. You can even microwave a POPpup™ to turn into a huge crackly treat.

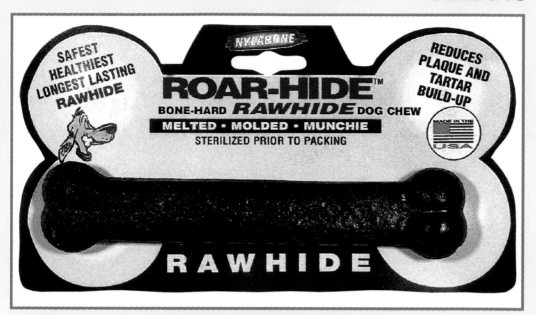

Roar-Hide® is completely edible and high in protein (over 86%) and low in fat (less than one-third of 1%). Unlike common rawhide, it is safer, less messy, and more fun for your Welsh Springer Spaniel.

need to be supplied via the food. Dogs are carnivores and this means their digestive tract has evolved to need a high quantity of meat as compared to humans. The digestive system of carnivores is unable to break down the tough cellulose walls of plant matter, but it is easily able to assimilate proteins from meat.

In order to gain its needed vegetable matter in a form that it can cope with, the carnivore eats all of its prey. This includes the partly digested food within the stomach. In commercially prepared foods, the cellulose is broken down by cooking. During this process the vitamin content is either greatly reduced or lost altogether. The manufacturer therefore adds vitamins once the heat process has been completed. This is why commercial foods are so useful as part of a feeding regimen, providing they are of good quality and from a company that has prepared the foods very carefully.

Proteins

These are made from amino acids, of which at least ten are essential if a puppy is to maintain healthy growth. Proteins provide the building blocks for the puppy's body. The richest sources are meat, fish and poultry, together with their by-products. The latter will include milk, cheese, yogurt, fishmeal, and eggs. Vegetable matter that has a high protein content includes soy beans, together with numerous

corn and other plant extracts that have been dehydrated. The actual protein content needed in the diet will be determined both by the activity level of the dog and his age. The total protein need will also be influenced by the digestibility factor of the food given.

Fats

These serve numerous roles in the puppy's body. They provide insulation against the cold, and help buffer the organs from knocks and general activity shocks. They provide the richest source of energy, and reserves of this, and they are vital in the transport of vitamins and other nutrients, via the blood, to all other organs. Finally, it is the fat content within a diet that gives it palatability. It is important that the fat content of a diet should not be excessive. This is because the high energy content of fats (more than twice that of protein or carbohydrate) will increase the overall energy content of the diet. The puppy will adjust its food intake to that of its energy needs, which are obviously more easily met in a high-energy diet. This will mean that while the fats are providing the energy needs of the puppy, the overall diet may not be providing its protein, vitamin, and mineral needs, so signs of protein deficiency will become apparent. Rich sources of fats are meat, their byproducts (butter, milk), and vegetable oils, such as safflower, olive, corn or soy bean.

Carrots are rich in fiber, carbohydrates and vitamin A. The CarrotBone™ by Nylabone® is a durable chew containing no plastics or artificial ingredients and it can be served as-is, in bone hard form, or microwaved to a biscuity consistency.

Carbohydrates

These are the principal energy compounds given to puppies and adult dogs. Their inclusion within most commercial brand dog foods is for cost, rather than dietary needs. These compounds are more commonly known as sugars, and they are seen in simple or complex compounds of carbon, hydrogen, and oxygen. One of the simple sugars is called glucose, and it is vital to many metabolic processes. When large chains of glucose are created, they form compound sugars. One of these is called glycogen, and it is found in the cells of animals. Another, called starch, is the material that is found in the cells of plants.

Vitamins

These are not foods as such but chemical compounds that assist in all aspects of an animal's life. They help in so many ways that to attempt to describe these

When you travel with your Welsh Springer Spaniel, bring his regular food along to avoid stomach upsets.

effectively would require a chapter in itself. Fruits are a rich source of vitamins, as is the liver of most animals. Many vitamins are unstable and easily destroyed by light, heat, moisture, or rancidity. An excess of vitamins, especially A and D, has been proven to be very harmful. Provided a puppy is receiving a balanced diet, it is most unlikely there will be a deficiency, whereas hypervitaminosis (an excess of vitamins) has become quite common due to owners and breeders feeding unneeded supplements. The only time you should feed extra vitamins to your puppy is if your veterinarian advises you to.

55

Minerals

These provide strength to bone and cell tissue, as well as assist in many metabolic processes. Examples are calcium, phosphorous, copper, iron, magnesium, selenium, potassium, zinc, and sodium. The recommended amounts of all minerals in the diet has not been fully established. Calcium and phosphorous are known to be important, especially to puppies. They help in forming strong bone. As with vitamins, a mineral deficiency is most unlikely in pups given a good and varied diet. Again, an excess can create problems—this applying equally to calcium.

Water

This is the most important of all nutrients, as is easily shown by the fact that the adult dog is made up of about 60 percent water, the puppy containing an even higher percentage. Dogs must retain a water balance, which means that the total intake should be balanced by the total output. The intake

Make sure your Welsh Springer Spaniel has cool clean water available to him at all times. Owners, Richard and Sandy Rohrbacher.

A Welsh Springer puppy will eat twice as much as an adult.

comes either by direct input (the tap or its equivalent), plus water released when food is oxidized, known as metabolic water (remember that all foods contain the elements hydrogen and oxygen that recombine in the body to create water). A dog without adequate water will lose condition more rapidly than one depleted of food, a fact common to most animal species.

AMOUNT TO FEED

The best way to determine dietary requirements is by observing the puppy's general health and physical appearance. If he is well covered with flesh, shows good bone development and muscle, and is an active alert puppy, then his diet is fine. A puppy will consume about twice as much as an adult (of the same breed). You should ask the breeder of your puppy to show you the amounts fed to their pups and this will be a good starting point.

The puppy should eat his meal in about five to seven minutes. Any leftover food can be discarded

57

or placed into the refrigerator until the next meal (but be sure it is thawed fully if your fridge is very cold).

If the puppy quickly devours its meal and is clearly still hungry, then you are not giving him enough food. If he eats readily but then begins to pick at it, or walks away leaving a quantity, then you are probably giving him too much food. Adjust this at the next meal and you will quickly begin to appreciate what the correct amount is. If, over a number of weeks, the pup starts to look fat, then he is obviously overeating; the reverse is true if he starts to look thin compared with others of the same breed.

WHEN TO FEED

It really does not matter what times of the day the puppy is fed, as long as he receives the needed quantity of food. Puppies from 8 weeks to 12 or 16 weeks need 3 or 4 meals a day. Older puppies and adult dogs should be fed twice a day. What is most important is that the feeding times are reasonably regular. They can be tailored to fit in with your own timetable—for example, 7 a.m. and 6 p.m. The dog will then expect his meals at these times each day. Keeping regular feeding times and feeding set amounts will help you monitor your puppy's or dog's health. If a dog that's normally enthusiastic about mealtimes and eats readily suddenly shows a lack of interest in food, you'll know something's not right.

Keeping your Welsh Springer on a regular feeding schedule will reduce his chances of stealing snacks in between meals and help you monitor what he eats.

TRAINING YOUR WELSH SPRINGER SPANIEL

Once your puppy has settled into your home and responds to his name, then you can begin his basic training. Before giving advice on how you should go about doing this, two important points should be made. You should train the puppy in isolation of any

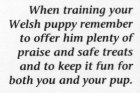
When training your Welsh puppy remember to offer him plenty of praise and safe treats and to keep it fun for both you and your pup.

potential distractions, and you should keep all lessons very short. It is essential that you have the full attention of your puppy. This is not possible if there are other people about, or televisions and radios on, or other pets in the vicinity. Even when the pup has become a young adult, the maximum time you should allocate to a lesson is about 20 minutes. However, you can give the puppy more than one lesson a day, three being as many as are recommended, each well spaced apart.

Before beginning a lesson, always play a little game with the puppy so he is in an active state of mind and thus more receptive to the matter at hand. Likewise, always end a lesson with fun-time for the pup,

Leash training your Welsh Springer is very important for his safety and for the safety of others. Fergie and Ruby bred by Barbara Smith take a walk together.

and always—this is most important—end on a high note, praising the puppy. Let the lesson end when the pup has done as you require so he receives lots of fuss. This will really build his confidence.

COLLAR AND LEASH TRAINING

Training a puppy to his collar and leash is very easy. Place a collar on the puppy and, although he will initially try to bite at it, he will soon forget it, the more so if you play with him. You can leave the collar on for a few hours. Some people leave their dogs' collars on all of the time, others only when they are taking the dog out. If it is to be left on, purchase a narrow or round one so it does not mark the fur.

Once the puppy ignores his collar, then you can attach the leash to it and let the puppy pull this along behind it for a few minutes. However, if the pup starts to chew at the leash, simply hold the leash but keep it slack and let the pup go where he wants. The idea is to let him get the feel of the leash, but not get in the habit of chewing it. Repeat this a couple of times a day for two days and the pup will get used to the leash without thinking that it will restrain him—which you will not have attempted to do yet.

Next, you can let the pup understand that the leash will restrict his movements. The first time he realizes this, he will pull and buck or just sit down. Immediately call the pup to you and give him lots of fuss. Never tug on the leash so the puppy is dragged along the floor, as this simply implants a negative thought in his mind.

THE COME COMMAND

Come is the most vital of all commands and especially so for the independently minded dog. To teach the puppy to come, let him reach the end of a long lead, then give the command and his name, gently pulling him toward you at the same time. As soon as he associates the word come with the action of moving toward you, pull only when he does not respond immediately. As he starts to come, move back to make him learn that he must come from a distance as well as when he is close to you. Soon you may be able to practice without a leash, but if he is slow to come or notably disobedient, go to him and

If you accustom your Welsh to wearing his collar when he is young, it will not bother him at all when he is older. Owners, Richard and Sandy Rohrbacher.

pull him toward you, repeating the command. Never scold a dog during this exercise—or any other exercise. Remember the trick is that the puppy must want to come to you. For the very independent dog, hand signals may work better than verbal commands.

THE SIT COMMAND

As with most basic commands, your puppy will learn this one in just a few lessons. You can give the puppy two lessons a day on the sit command but he will make just as much progress with one 15-minute lesson each day. Some trainers will advise you that you should not proceed to other commands until the previous one has been learned really well. However, a bright young pup is quite capable of handling more than one command per lesson, and certainly per day. Indeed, as time progresses, you will be going through each command as a matter of routine before a new one is attempted. This is so the puppy always starts, as well as ends, a lesson on a high note, having successfully completed something.

Call the puppy to you and fuss over him. Place one hand on his hindquarters and the other under his upper chest. Say "Sit" in a pleasant (never harsh) voice. At the same time, push down his rear end and push up under his chest. Now lavish praise on the puppy. Repeat this a few times and your pet will get the idea. Once the puppy is in the sit position you will release your hands. At first he will tend to get up, so immediately repeat the exercise. The lesson will end when the pup is in the sit position. When the puppy understands the command, and does it right away, you can slowly move backwards so that you are a few feet away from him. If he attempts to come to you, simply place him back in the original position and start again. Do not attempt to keep the pup in the sit position for too long. At this age, even a few seconds is a long while and you do not want him to get bored with lessons before he has even begun them.

THE HEEL COMMAND

All dogs should be able to walk nicely on a leash without their owners being involved in a tug-of-war. The heel command will follow leash training. Heel training is best done where you have a wall to one side of you. This will restrict the puppy's lateral movements, so you only have to contend with forward and backward situations. A fence is an alternative, or you can do the lesson in the garage. Again, it is better to do the lesson in private, not on a public sidewalk where there will be many distractions.

With a puppy, there will be no need to use a choke collar as you can be just as effective with a regular one. The leash should be of good length, certainly not too short. You can adjust the space between you, the puppy, and the wall so your pet has only a small amount of room to move sideways. This being so, he will either hang back or pull ahead—the latter is the more desirable state as it indicates a bold pup who is not frightened of you.

Hold the leash in your right hand and pass it through your left. As the puppy moves ahead and strains on the leash, give the leash a quick jerk backwards with your left hand, at the same time saying "Heel." The position you want the pup to be in is such that his chest is level with, or just behind, an imaginary line from your knee. When the puppy is in this position, praise him and begin walking again, and the whole exercise will be repeated. Once the puppy begins to get the message, you can use your left hand to pat the side of your knee so the pup is encouraged to keep close to your side.

Your Welsh Springer puppy will look to you, his owner, for the care and guidance he needs to become a well-mannered adult. Owner, Linda Brennan.

It is useful to suddenly do an about-turn when the pup understands the basics. The puppy will now be behind you, so you can pat your knee and say "Heel." As soon as the pup is in the correct position, give him lots of praise. The puppy will now be beginning to associate certain words with certain actions. Whenever he is not in the heel position he will experience displeasure as you jerk the leash, but when he comes alongside you he will receive praise. Given these two options, he will always prefer the latter—assuming he has no other reason to fear you, which would then create a dilemma in his mind.

Once the lesson has been well learned, then you can adjust your pace from a slow walk to a quick one and the puppy will come to adjust. The slow walk is always the more difficult for most puppies, as they are usually anxious to be on the move.

If you have no wall to walk against then things will be a little more difficult because the pup will tend to wander to his left. This means you need to give lateral jerks as well as bring the pup to your side. End the lesson when the pup is walking nicely beside you. Begin the lesson with a few sit commands (which he understands by now), so you're starting with success and praise. If your puppy is nervous on the leash, you should never drag him to your side as you may see so many other people do (who obviously didn't invest in a good book like you did!). If the pup sits down, call him to your side and give lots of praise. The pup must always come to you because he wants to. If he is dragged to your side he will see you doing the dragging—a big negative. When he races ahead he does not see you jerk the leash, so all he knows is that something restricted his movement and, once he was in a given position, you gave him lots of praise. This is using canine psychology to your advantage.

Always try to remember that if a dog must be disciplined, then try not to let him associate the discipline with you. This is not possible in all matters but, where it is, this is definitely to be preferred.

THE STAY COMMAND

This command follows from the sit. Face the puppy and say "Sit." Now step backwards, and as you do, say "Stay." Let the pup remain in the position for only a few seconds before calling him to you and giving lots of praise. Repeat this, but step further back. You do not need to shout at the puppy. Your pet is not deaf; in fact, his hearing is far better than yours. Speak just loudly enough for the pup to hear, yet use a firm voice. You can stretch the word to form a "sta-a-a-y." If the pup gets up and comes to you simply lift him up, place him back in the original position, and start again. As the pup comes to understand the command, you can move further and further back.

The next test is to walk away after placing the pup. This will mean your back is to him, which will tempt him to follow you. Keep an eye over your shoulder, and the minute the pup starts to move, spin around and, using a sterner voice, say either "Sit" or "Stay." If the pup has gotten quite close to you, then, again, return him to the original position.

As the weeks go by you can increase the length of time the pup is left in the stay position—but two to three minutes is quite long enough for a puppy. If your puppy drops into a lying position and is clearly more comfortable, there is nothing wrong with this. Likewise, your pup will want to face the direction in which you walked off. Some trainers will insist that the dog faces the direction he was placed in, regardless of whether you move off on his blind side. I have never believed in this sort of obedience because it has no practical benefit.

THE DOWN COMMAND

From the puppy's viewpoint, the down command can be one of the more difficult ones to accept. This is because the position is one taken up by a submissive dog in a wild pack situation. A timid dog will roll over—a natural gesture of submission. A bolder pup

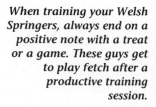

When training your Welsh Springers, always end on a positive note with a treat or a game. These guys get to play fetch after a productive training session.

will want to get up, and might back off, not feeling he should have to submit to this command. He will feel that he is under attack from you and about to be punished—which is what would be the position in his natural environment. Once he comes to understand this is not the case, he will accept this unnatural position without any problem.

You may notice that some dogs will sit very quickly, but will respond to the down command more slowly— it is their way of saying that they will obey the command, but under protest!

There two ways to teach this command. One is, in my mind, more intimidating than the other, but it is up to you to decide which one works best for you. The first method is to stand in front of your puppy and bring him to the sit position, with his collar and leash on. Pass the leash under your left foot so that when you pull on it, the result is that the pup's neck is forced downwards. With your free left hand, push the pup's shoulders down while at the same time saying "Down."

This is when a bold pup will instantly try to back off and wriggle in full protest. Hold the pup firmly by the shoulders so he stays in the position for a second or two, then tell him what a good dog he is and give him lots of praise. Repeat this only a few times in a lesson because otherwise the puppy will get bored and upset over this command. End with an easy command that brings back the pup's confidence.

The second method, and the one I prefer, is done as follows: Stand in front of the pup and then tell him to sit. Now kneel down, which is immediately far less intimidating to the puppy than to have you towering above him. Take each of his front legs and pull them forward, at the same time saying "Down." Release the legs and quickly apply light pressure on the shoulders with your left hand. Then, as quickly, say "Good boy" and give lots of fuss. Repeat two or three times only. The pup will learn over a few lessons. Remember, this is a very submissive act on the pup's behalf, so there is no need to rush matters.

RECALL TO HEEL COMMAND

When your puppy is coming to the heel position from an off-leash situation—such as if he has been running free—he should do this in the correct manner. He should pass behind you and take up his position and then sit. To teach this command, have the pup in front of you in the sit position with his collar and leash on. Hold the leash

A well-trained Welsh Springer Spaniel will be welcomed in anyone's home. This group of Welsh are attending a Christmas party. Owners, S. O'Neill, B. and R. Smith, M. Daniel, B. Orishak, L. Brennan, and R. Stover.

in your right hand. Give him the command to heel, and pat your left knee. As the pup starts to move forward, use your right hand to guide him behind you. If need be you can hold his collar and walk the dog around the back of you to the desired position. You will need to repeat this a few times until the dog understands what is wanted.

When he has done this a number of times, you can try it without the collar and leash. If the pup comes up toward your left side, then bring him to the sit position in front of you, hold his collar and walk him around the back of you. He will eventually understand and automatically pass around your back each time. If the dog is already behind you when you recall him, then he should automatically come to your left side, which you will be patting with your hand.

Welsh Springer Spaniels have excellent noses and love to participate in outdoor sports, making it easy for them to excel at tracking and hunting.

THE NO COMMAND

This is a command that must be obeyed every time without fail. There are no halfway stages, he must be 100-percent reliable. Most delinquent dogs have never been taught this command; included in these are the jumpers, the barkers, and the biters. Were your puppy to approach a poisonous snake or any other potential danger, the no command, coupled with the recall, could save his life. You do not need to give a specific lesson for this command because it will crop up time and again in day-to-day life.

If the puppy is chewing a slipper, you should approach the pup, take hold of the slipper, and say "No" in a stern voice. If he jumps onto the furniture, lift him off and say "No" and place him gently on the floor. You must be consistent in the use of the command and apply it every time he is doing something you do not want him to do.

YOUR HEALTHY WELSH SPRINGER SPANIEL

Dogs, like all other animals, are capable of contracting problems and diseases that, in most cases, are easily avoided by sound husbandry—meaning well-bred and well-cared-for animals are less prone to developing diseases and problems than are carelessly bred and neglected animals. Your knowledge of how to avoid problems is far more valuable than all of the books and advice on how to cure them. Respectively, the only person you should listen to about treatment is your vet. Veterinarians don't have all the answers, but at least they are trained to analyze and treat illnesses, and are aware of the full implications of treatments. This does not mean a few old remedies aren't good standbys when all else fails, but in most cases modern science provides the best treatments for disease.

Opposite: Veterinarians are trained to analyze and treat illnesses. Having complete trust in your chosen veterinarian is tantamount to the long life of your dog.

PHYSICAL EXAMS

Your puppy should receive regular physical examinations or check-ups. These come in two forms. One is obviously performed by your vet, and the other is a day-to-day procedure that should be done by you. Apart from the fact the exam will highlight any problem at an early stage, it is an excellent way of socializing the pup to being handled.

To do the physical exam yourself, start at the head and work your way around the body. You are looking for any sign of lesions, or any indication of parasites on the pup. The most common parasites are fleas and ticks.

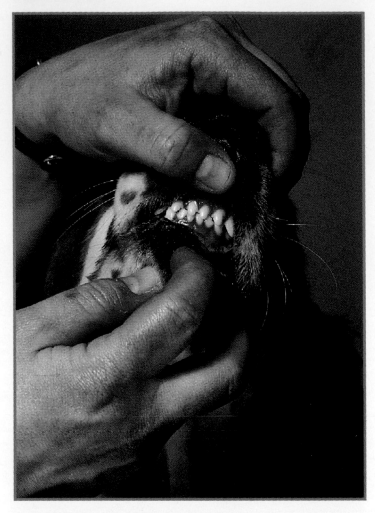

A thorough oral exam should be a part of your Welsh Springer's regular check-up.

HEALTHY TEETH AND GUMS

Chewing is instinctual. Puppies chew so that their teeth and jaws grow strong and healthy as they develop. As the permanent teeth begin to emerge, it is painful and annoying to the puppy, and puppy owners must recognize that their new charges need something safe upon which to chew. Unfortunately, once the puppy's permanent teeth have emerged and settled solidly into the jaw, the chewing instinct does not fade. Adult dogs instinctively need to clean their teeth, massage their gums, and exercise their jaws through chewing.

It is necessary for your dog to have clean teeth. You should take your dog to the veterinarian at least once a year to have his teeth cleaned and to have his mouth examined for any sign of oral disease. Although dogs do not get cavities in the same way humans do, dogs'

The Hercules® by Nylabone® has raised dental tips that help fight plaque on your Welsh Springer Spaniel's teeth and gums.

teeth accumulate tartar, and more quickly than humans do! Veterinarians recommend brushing your dog's teeth daily. But who can find time to brush their dog's teeth daily? The accumulation of tartar and plaque on our dog's teeth when not removed can cause irritation and eventually erode the enamel and finally destroy the teeth. Advanced cases, while destroying the teeth, bring on gingivitis and periodontitis, two very serious conditions that can affect the dog's internal organs as well...to say nothing about bad breath!

Since everyone can't brush their dog's teeth daily or get to the veterinarian often enough for him to scale

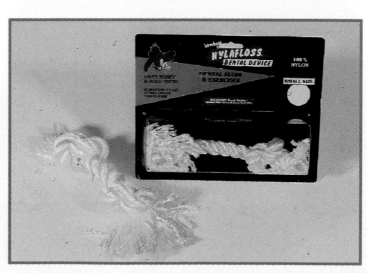

Nylafloss® does wonders for your Welsh Springer Spaniel's dental health by massaging his gums and literally flossing between his teeth, loosening plaque and tartar build-up. Unlike cotton tug toys, Nylafloss® won't rot or fray.

the dog's teeth, providing the dog with something safe to chew on will help maintain oral hygeine. Chew devices from Nylabone® keep dogs' teeth clean, but they also provide an excellent resource for entertainment and relief of doggie tensions. Nylabone® products give your dog something to do for an hour or two every day and during that hour or two, your dog will be taking an active part in keeping his teeth and gums healthy…without even realizing it! That's invaluable to your dog, and valuable to you!

Nylabone® provides fun bones, challenging bones, and *safe* bones. It is an owner's responsibility to recognize safe chew toys from dangerous ones. Your dog will chew and devour anything you give him. Dogs must not be permitted to chew on items that they can break. Pieces of broken objects can do internal damage to a dog, besides ripping the dog's mouth. Cheap plastic or rubber toys can cause stoppage in the intestines; such stoppages are operable only if caught immediately.

The most obvious choices, in this case, may be the worst choice. Natural beef bones were not designed for chewing and cannot take too much pressure from the sides. Due to the abrasive nature of these bones, they should be offered most sparingly. Knuckle bones, though once very popular for dogs, can be easily

Nylabone® is the only plastic dog bone made of 100% virgin nylon, specially processed to create a tough, durable, completely safe bone.

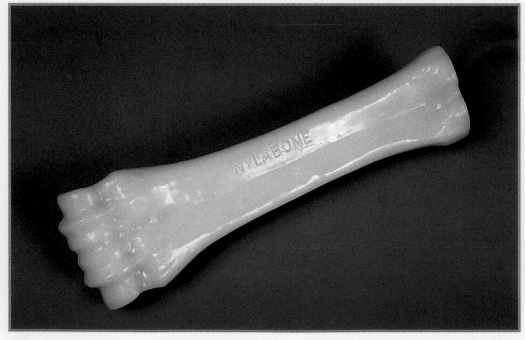

Chick-n-Cheez Chooz® are completely safe and nutritious health chews made from pure cheese protein, chicken, and fortified with vitamin E. They contain no salt, sugar, plastic, or preservatives and less than 1% fat.

chewed up and eaten by dogs. At the very least, digestion is interrupted; at worst, the dog can choke or suffer from intestinal blockage.

When a dog chews hard on a Nylabone®, little bristle-like projections appear on the surface of the bone. These help to clean the dog's teeth and add to the gum-massaging. Given the chemistry of the nylon, the bristle can pass through the dog's intestinal tract without effect. Since nylon is inert, no microorganism can grow on it, and it can be washed in soap and water or sterilized in boiling water or in an autoclave.

For the sake of your dog, his teeth and your own peace of mind, provide your dog with Nylabones®. They have 100 variations from which to choose.

FIGHTING FLEAS

Fleas are very mobile and may be red, black, or brown in color. The adults suck the blood of the host, while the larvae feed on the feces of the adults, which is rich in blood. Flea "dirt" may be seen on the pup as very tiny clusters of blackish specks that look like freshly ground pepper. The eggs of fleas may be laid on the puppy, though they are more commonly laid off the host in a favorable place, such as the bedding. They normally hatch in 4 to 21 days, depending on the temperature, but they can survive for up to 18 months if temperature conditions are not favorable. The larvae are maggot-like and molt a couple of times before forming pupae, which can survive long periods until the temperature, or the vibration of a nearby host, causes them to emerge and jump on a host.

There are a number of effective treatments available, and you should discuss them with your veterinarian, then follow all instructions for the one you choose. Any treatment will involve a product for your puppy or dog and one for the environment, and will require diligence on your part to treat all areas and thoroughly clean your home and yard until the infestation is eradicated.

THE TROUBLE WITH TICKS

Ticks are arthropods of the spider family, which means they have eight legs (though the larvae have six). They bury their headparts into the host and gorge on its blood. They are easily seen as small grain-like creatures sticking out from the skin. They are often picked up when dogs play in fields, but may also arrive in your yard via wild animals—even birds—or stray cats and dogs. Some ticks are species-specific, others are more adaptable and will host on many species.

The cat flea is the most common flea of dogs. It starts feeding soon after it makes contact with the dog.

The deer tick is the most common carrier of Lyme disease. Photo courtesy of Virbac Laboratories, Inc., Fort Worth, Texas.

The most troublesome type of tick is the deer tick, which spreads the deadly Lyme disease that can cripple a dog (or a person). Deer ticks are tiny and very hard to detect. Often, by the time they're big enough to notice, they've been feeding on the dog for a few days—long enough to do their damage. Lyme disease was named for the area of the United States in which it was first detected—Lyme, Connecticut—but has now been diagnosed in almost all parts of the U.S. Your veterinarian can advise you of the danger to your dog(s) in your area, and may suggest your dog be vaccinated for Lyme. Always go over your dog with a fine-toothed flea comb when you come in from walking through any area that may harbor deer ticks, and if your dog is acting unusually sluggish or sore, seek veterinary advice.

Attempts to pull a tick free will invariably leave the headpart in the pup, where it will die and cause an infected wound or abscess. The best way to remove ticks is to dab a strong saline solution, iodine, or alcohol on them. This will numb them, causing them to loosen their hold, at which time they can be removed with forceps. The wound can then be cleaned and covered with an antiseptic ointment. If ticks are common in your area, consult with your vet for a suitable pesticide to be used in kennels, on bedding, and on the puppy or dog.

INSECTS AND OTHER OUTDOOR DANGERS

There are many biting insects, such as mosquitoes, that can cause discomfort to a puppy. Many diseases are transmitted by the males of these species.

A pup can easily get a grass seed or thorn lodged between his pads or in the folds of his ears. These may go unnoticed until an abscess forms.

This is where your daily check of the puppy or dog will do a world of good. If your puppy has been playing in long grass or places where there may be thorns, pine needles, wild animals, or parasites, the check-up is a wise precaution.

After a romp outdoors, be sure check your Welsh Springer Spaniel's coat for fleas and ticks. Owner, Caroline Kaplonski.

SKIN DISORDERS

Apart from problems associated with lesions created by biting pests, a puppy may fall foul to a number of other skin disorders. Examples are ringworm, mange, and eczema. Ringworm is not caused by a worm, but is a fungal infection. It manifests itself as a sore-looking bald circle. If your puppy should have any form of bald patches, let your veterinarian check him over; a microscopic examination can confirm the condition. Many old remedies for ringworm exist, such as iodine, carbolic acid, formalin, and other tinctures, but modern drugs are superior.

Fungal infections can be very difficult to treat, and even more difficult to eradicate, because of the spores. These can withstand most treatments, other than burning, which is the best thing to do with bedding once the condition has been confirmed.

Mange is a general term that can be applied to many skin conditions where the hair falls out and a flaky crust develops and falls away.

Often, dogs will scratch themselves, and this invariably is worse than the original condition, for it opens lesions that are then subject to viral, fungal, or parasitic attack. The cause of the problem can be various species of mites. These either live on skin debris and the hair follicles, which they destroy, or they bury themselves just beneath the skin and feed on the tissue. Applying general remedies from pet stores is not recommended because it is essential to identify the type of mange before a specific treatment is effective.

Eczema is another non-specific term applied to many skin disorders. The condition can be brought about in many ways. Sunburn, chemicals, allergies to foods, drugs, pollens, and even stress can all produce a deterioration of the skin and coat. Given the range of causal factors, treatment can be difficult because the problem is one of identification. It is a case of taking each possibility at a time and trying to correctly diagnose the matter. If the cause is of a dietary nature then you must remove one item at a time in order to find out if the dog is allergic to a given food. It could, of course, be the lack of a nutrient that is the problem, so if the condition persists, you should consult your veterinarian.

INTERNAL DISORDERS

It cannot be overstressed that it is very foolish to attempt to diagnose an internal disorder without the advice of a veterinarian. Take a relatively common problem such as diarrhea. It might be caused by nothing more serious than the puppy hogging a lot of food or eating something that it has never previously eaten. Conversely, it could be the first indication of a potentially fatal disease. It's up to your veterinarian to make the correct diagnosis.

The following symptoms, especially if they accompany each other or are progressively added to earlier symptoms, mean you should visit the veterinarian right away:

Continual vomiting. All dogs vomit from time to time and this is not necessarily a sign of illness. They will eat grass to induce vomiting. It is a natural cleansing process common to many carnivores. However, continued vomiting is a clear sign of a problem. It may be a blockage in the pup's intestinal tract, it may be induced by worms, or it could be due to any number of diseases.

Diarrhea. This, too, may be nothing more than a temporary condition due to many factors. Even a change of home can induce diarrhea, because this often stresses the pup, and invariably there is some change in the diet. If it persists more than 48 hours then something is amiss. If blood is seen in the feces, waste no time at all in taking the dog to the vet.

Running eyes and/or nose. A pup might have a chill and this will cause the eyes and nose to weep. Again, this should quickly clear up if the puppy is placed in a warm environment and away from any drafts. If it does not, and especially if a mucous discharge is seen, then the pup has an illness that must be diagnosed.

Coughing. Prolonged coughing is a sign of a problem, usually of a respiratory nature.

Wheezing. If the pup has difficulty breathing and makes a wheezing sound when breathing, then something is wrong.

Cries when attempting to defecate or urinate. This might only be a minor problem due to the hard state of the feces, but it could be more serious, especially if the pup cries when urinating.

Cries when touched. Obviously, if you do not handle a puppy with care he might yelp. However, if he cries even when lifted gently, then he has an internal problem that becomes apparent when pressure is applied to a given area of the body. Clearly, this must be diagnosed.

Refuses food. Generally, puppies and dogs are greedy creatures when it comes to feeding time. Some might be more fussy, but none should refuse more than one meal. If they go for a number of hours without showing any interest in their food, then something is not as it should be.

General listlessness. All puppies have their off days when they do not seem their usual cheeky, mischievous selves. If this condition persists for more than two days then there is little doubt of a problem. They may not show any of the signs listed, other than perhaps a reduced interest in their food. There are many diseases that can develop internally without displaying obvious clinical signs. Blood, fecal, and other tests are needed in order to identify the disorder before it reaches an advanced state that may not be treatable.

WORMS

There are many species of worms, and a number of these live in the tissues of dogs and most other animals. Many create no problem at all, so you are not even aware they exist. Others can be tolerated in small levels, but become a major problem if they number more than a few. The most common types seen in dogs are roundworms and tapeworms. While roundworms are the greater problem, tapeworms require an intermediate host so are more easily eradicated.

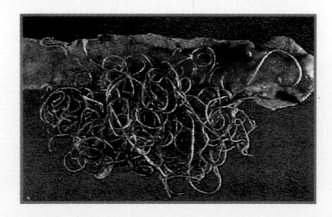

Roundworms are spaghetti-like worms that cause a pot-bellied appearance and dull coat, along with more severe symptoms, such as diarrhea and vomiting. Photo courtesy of Merck AgVet.

Roundworms of the species *Toxocara canis* infest the dog. They may grow to a length of 8 inches (20 cm) and look like strings of spaghetti. The worms feed on the digesting food in the pup's intestines. In chronic cases the puppy will become pot-bellied, have diarrhea, and will vomit. Eventually, he will stop eating, having passed through the stage when he always seems hungry. The worms lay eggs in the puppy and these pass out in his feces. They are then either ingested by the pup, or they are eaten by mice, rats, or beetles. These may then be eaten by the puppy and the life cycle is complete.

Larval worms can migrate to the womb of a pregnant bitch, or to her mammary glands, and this is how they pass to the puppy. The pregnant bitch can be wormed, which will help. The pups can, and should,

Whipworms are hard to find unless you strain your dog's feces, and this is best left to a veterinarian. Pictured here are adult whipworms.

be wormed when they are about two weeks old. Repeat worming every 10 to 14 days and the parasites should be removed. Worms can be extremely dangerous to young puppies, so you should be sure the pup is wormed as a matter of routine.

Tapeworms can be seen as tiny rice-like eggs sticking to the puppy's or dog's anus. They are less destructive, but still undesirable. The eggs are eaten by mice, fleas, rabbits, and other animals that serve as intermediate hosts. They develop into a larval stage and the host must be eaten by the dog in order to complete the chain. Your vet will supply a suitable remedy if tapeworms are seen or suspected. There are other worms, such as hookworms and whipworms, that are also blood suckers. They will make a pup anemic, and blood might be seen in the feces, which can be examined by the vet to confirm their presence. Cleanliness in all matters is the best preventative measure for all worms.

Heartworm infestation in dogs is passed by mosquitoes but can be prevented by a monthly (or daily) treatment that is given orally. Talk to your vet about the risk of heartworm in your area.

BLOAT (GASTRIC DILATATION)

This condition has proved fatal in many dogs, especially large and deep-chested breeds, such as the Weimaraner and the Great Dane. However, any dog can get bloat. It is caused by swallowing air during exercise, food/water gulping or another strenuous task. As many believe, it is not the result of flatulence. The stomach of an affected dog twists, disallowing food and blood flow and resulting in harmful toxins being released into the bloodstream. Death can easily follow if the condition goes undetected.

The best preventative measure is not to feed large meals or exercise your puppy or dog immediately after he has eaten. Veterinarians recommend feeding three smaller meals per day in an elevated feeding rack, adding water to dry food to prevent gulping, and not offering water during mealtimes.

VACCINATIONS

Every puppy, purebred or mixed breed, should be vaccinated against the major canine diseases. These are distemper, leptospirosis, hepatitis, and canine parvovirus. Your puppy may have received a temporary vaccination against distemper before you purchased him, but be sure to ask the breeder to be sure.

The age at which vaccinations are given can vary, but will usually be when the pup is 8 to 12 weeks old. By this time any protection given to the pup by antibodies received from his mother via her initial milk feeds will be losing their strength.

Rely on your veterinarian for the most effectual vaccination schedule for your Welsh Springer Spaniel puppy.

The puppy's immune system works on the basis that the white blood cells engulf and render harmless

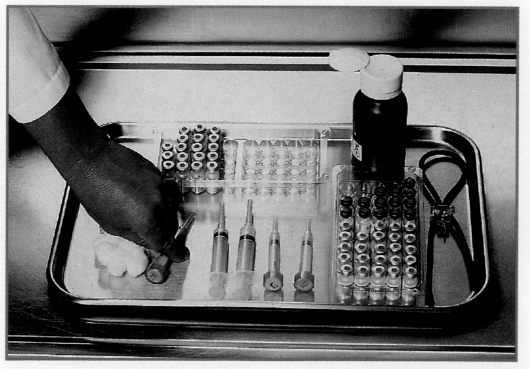

attacking bacteria. However, they must first recognize a potential enemy.

Vaccines are either dead bacteria or they are live, but in very small doses. Either type prompts the pup's defense system to attack them. When a large attack then comes (if it does), the immune system recognizes it and massive numbers of lymphocytes (white blood corpuscles) are mobilized to counter the attack. However, the ability of the cells to recognize these dangerous viruses can diminish over a period of time. It is therefore useful to provide annual reminders about the nature of the enemy. This is done by means of booster injections that keep the immune system on its alert. Immunization is not 100-percent guaranteed to be successful, but is very close. Certainly it is better than giving the puppy no protection.

Dogs are subject to other viral attacks, and if these are of a high-risk factor in your area, then your vet will suggest you have the puppy vaccinated against these as well.

Your puppy or dog should also be vaccinated against the deadly rabies virus. In fact, in many places it is illegal for your dog not to be vaccinated. This is to protect your dog, your family, and the rest of the animal population from this deadly virus that infects the nervous system and causes dementia and death.

ACCIDENTS

All puppies will get their share of bumps and bruises due to the rather energetic way they play. These will usually heal themselves over a few days. Small cuts should be bathed with a suitable disinfectant and then smeared with an antiseptic ointment. If a cut looks more serious, then stem the flow of blood with a towel or makeshift tourniquet and rush the pup to the veterinarian. Never apply so much pressure to the wound that it might restrict the flow of blood to the limb.

In the case of burns you should apply cold water or an ice pack to the surface. If the burn was due to a chemical, then this must be washed away with copious amounts of water. Apply petroleum jelly, or any vegetable oil, to the burn. Trim away the hair if need be. Wrap the dog in a blanket and rush him to the vet. The pup may go into shock, depending on the severity of the burn, and this will result in a lowered blood pressure, which is dangerous and the reason the pup must receive immediate veterinary attention.

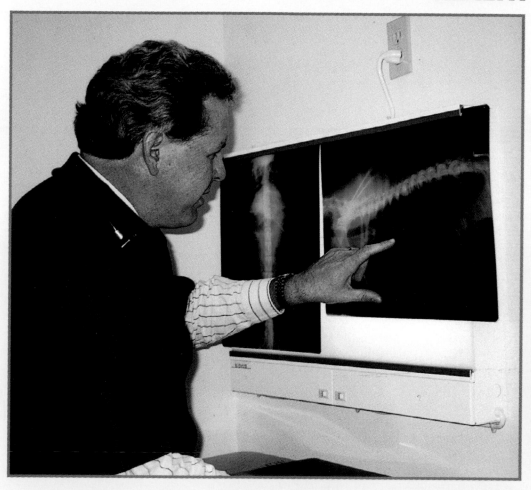

It is a good idea to x-ray the chest and abdomen on any dog hit by a car.

If a broken limb is suspected then try to keep the animal as still as possible. Wrap your pup or dog in a blanket to restrict movement and get him to the veterinarian as soon as possible. Do not move the dog's head so it is tilting backward, as this might result in blood entering the lungs.

Do not let your pup jump up and down from heights, as this can cause considerable shock to the joints. Like all youngsters, puppies do not know when enough is enough, so you must do all their thinking for them.

Provided you apply strict hygiene to all aspects of raising your puppy, and you make daily checks on his physical state, you have done as much as you can to safeguard him during his most vulnerable period. Routine visits to your veterinarian are also recommended, especially while the puppy is under one year of age. The vet may notice something that did not seem important to you.

CONGENITAL AND ACQUIRED DISORDERS

by Judy Iby, RVT

Veterinarians and breeders now recognize that many of the disease processes and faults in dogs, as well as in human beings, have a genetic predisposition. These faults are found not only in the purebred dog but in the mixed breed as well. Likely these diseases have been present for decades but more recently are being identified and attributed to inheritance. Fortunately many of these problems are not life threatening or even debilitating. Many of these disorders have a low incidence. It is true that some breeds and some bloodlines within a breed have a higher frequency than others. It is always wise to discuss this subject with breeders of your breed.

Presently very few of the hundreds of disorders can be identified through genetic testing. Hopefully with today's technology and the desire to improve our breeding stock, genetic testing will become more readily available. In the meantime the reputable breeder does the recommended testing for his breed. The American Kennel Club is encouraging OFA (Orthopedic Foundation for Animals) hip and elbow certification and CERF (Canine Eye Registration Foundation) certifications and is listing them on AKC registrations and pedigrees. This is a step forward for the AKC in encouraging better breeding. They also founded a Canine Health Foundation to aid in the research of diseases in the purebred dog.

Opposite: The responsible Welsh Springer Spaniel breeder, understanding the potential problems within the breed, strives to produce healthy puppies and contribute to the betterment of the breed.

BONES AND JOINTS

Hip Dysplasia

Canine hip dysplasia has been confirmed in 79 breeds. It is the malformation of the hip joint's ball and socket, with clinical signs from none to severe hip lameness. It may appear as early as five months. The incidence is

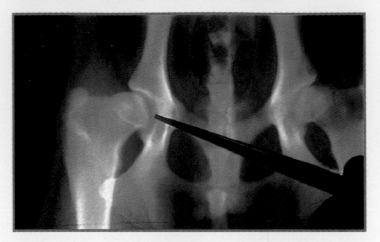

Radiograph of a dog with hip dysplasia. Note the flattened femoral head at the marker. Photo courtesy of Toronto Academy of Veterinary Medicine, Toronto, Canada.

reduced within a bloodline by breeding normal to normal, generation after generation. Upon submitting normal pelvic radiographs, the OFA will issue a certification number.

Elbow Dysplasia

Elbow dysplasia results from abnormal development of the ulna, one of the bones of the upper arm. During bone growth, a small area of bone (the anconeal process) fails to fuse with the rest of the bone. This results in an unstable elbow joint and lameness, which is aggravated by exercise. OFA certifies free of this disorder.

Patellar Luxation

This condition can be medial or lateral. Breeders call patellar luxations "slips" for "slipped kneecaps." OFA offers a registry for this disorder. Patellar luxations may or may not cause problems.

Intervertebral Disk Disease (IVD)

IVD is a condition in which a disk(s), the cushion between each vertebrae of the spine, tears and the gel-like material leaks out and presses on the spinal cord. The degeneration is progressive, starting as early as two to nine months, but usually the neurological symptoms are not apparent until three to six years of age. Symptoms include pain, paresis (weariness), incoordination, and paralysis. IVD is a medical emergency. If you are unable to get professional care immediately, then confine your dog to a crate or small area until he can be seen.

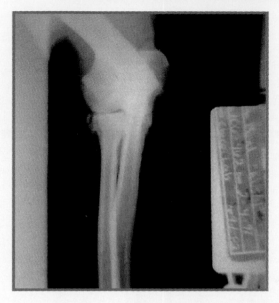

Fragmented coronoid process of the elbow, a manifestation of elbow dysplasia. Photo courtesy of Jack Henry.

Spondylitis

Usually seen in middle to old-age dogs and potentially quite serious in the latter, spondylitis is inflammation of the vertebral joints and degeneration of intervertebral disks resulting in bony spur-like outgrowths that may fuse.

CARDIOVASCULAR AND LYMPHATIC SYSTEMS

Dilated Cardiomyopathy

Prevalent in several breeds, this is a disease in which the heart muscle is damaged or destroyed to the point that it cannot pump blood properly through the body resulting in signs of heart failure. Diagnosis is confirmed by cardiac ultrasound.

Lymphosarcoma

This condition can occur in young dogs but usually appears in dogs over the age of five years. Symptoms include fever, weight loss, anorexia, painless enlargement of the lymph nodes, and nonspecific signs of illness. It is the most common type of cancer found in dogs. Chemotherapy treatment will prolong the dog's life but will not cure the disease at this time.

BLOOD

Von Willebrand's Disease

VWD has been confirmed in over 50 breeds and is

a manageable disease. It is characterized by moderate to severe bleeding, corrected by blood transfusions from normal dogs and frequently seen with hypothyroidism. When levels are low, a pre-surgical blood transfusion may be necessary. Many breeders screen their breeding stock for vWD.

Immune-Mediated Blood Disease

Immune-mediated diseases affect the red blood cells and platelets. They are called autoimmune hemolytic anemia or immune-mediated anemia when red blood cells are affected, and autoimmune thrombocytopenic purpura, idiopathic thrombocytopenic purpura, and immune-mediated thrombocytopenia when platelets are involved. The disease may appear acutely. Symptoms include jaundice (yellow color) of the gums and eyes and dark brown or dark red urine. Symptoms of platelet disease include pinpoint bruises or hemorrhages in the skin, gums and eye membranes; nosebleeds; bleeding from the GI tract or into the urine. Any of these symptoms constitutes an emergency!

DIGESTIVE SYSTEM AND ORAL CAVITY

Colitis

This disorder has no known cause and appears with some frequency in certain breeds. It is characterized by an intermittent bloody stool, with or without diarrhea.

Chronic Hepatitis

This is the result of liver failure occuring at relatively young ages. In many cases clinical signs are apparent for less than two weeks. They include anorexia, lethargy, vomiting, depression, diarrhea, trembling or shaking, excess thirst and urination, weight loss, and dark bloody stool. Early diagnosis and treatment promise the best chance for survival.

Copper Toxicity

Copper toxicity occurs when excessive copper is concentrated in the liver. In 1995 there was a breakthrough when the DNA marker was identified in one of the afflicted breeds. Therefore carriers will be identified in the future.

ENDOCRINE SYSTEM

Hypothyroidism

Over 50 breeds have been diagnosed with hypothyroidism. It is the number-one endocrine disorder in the dog and is the result of an underactive thyroid gland. Conscientious breeders are screening their dogs if the disease is common to their breed or bloodline. The critical years for the decline of thyroid function are usually between three and eight, although it can appear at an older age. A simple blood test can diagnose or rule out this disorder. It is easily and inexpensively treated by giving thyroid replacement therapy daily. Untreated hypothyroidism can be devastating to your dog.

Addison's Disease

Primary adrenal insufficiency is caused by damage to the adrenal cortex, and secondary adrenocortical insufficiency is the result of insufficient production of the hormone ACTH by the pituitary gland. Symptoms may include depression, anorexia, a weak femoral pulse, vomiting or diarrhea, weakness, dehydration, and occasionally bradycardia.

Cushing's Disease

Hyperadrenocorticism is the over-production of steroid hormone. Dogs on steroid therapy may show Cushing-like symptoms. Some of the symptoms are excess thirst and urination, hair loss, and an enlarged, pendulous, or flaccid abdomen.

EYES

Cataracts

Breeders should screen their breeding stock for this disorder. A cataract is defined as any opacity of the lens or its capsule. It may progress and produce blindness or it may remain small and cause no clinical impairment of vision. Unfortunately some inherited cataracts appear later in life after the dog has already been bred.

Lens Luxation

This condition results when the lens of the eye is not in normal position, and may result in secondary glaucoma.

Glaucoma

Primary glaucoma is caused by increased intraocular pressure due to inadequate aqueous drainage and is not associated with other intraocular diseases. It may initially be in one eye. Secondary glaucoma is caused by increased intraocular pressure brought on by another ocular disease, tumor, or inflammation.

Keratoconjunctivitis Sicca

"Dry eye" (the decrease in production of tears) may be the result of a congenital or inherited deficiency of the aqueous layer, a lack of the proper nervous stimulation of the tearing system, a traumatic incident, or drugs, including topical anesthetics (such as

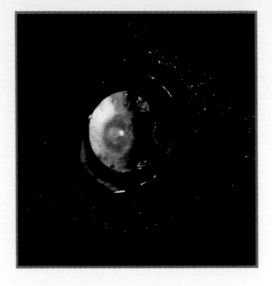

An immature cataract is evident in this dilated pupil. The central white area and cloudy areas at 4:00, 6:00 and 8:00 represent the cataract. Photo courtesy of Dr. Kerry L. Ketring.

atropine, and antibiotics containing sulfadiazine, phenazopyridine or salicyla-sulfapyridine). There seems to be an increased incidence of "dry eye" after "cherry eye" removal.

Progressive Retinal Atrophy (PRA)

This is the progressive loss of vision, first at night, followed by total blindness. It is inherited in many breeds.

Distichiasis

Distichiasis results from extra rows of eyelashes growing out of the meibomian gland ducts. This condition may cause tearing, but tearing may be the result of some other problem that needs to be investigated.

Entropion
Entropion is the inward rolling of the eyelid, usually lower lid, which can cause inflammation and may need surgical correction.

Ectropion
Ectropion is the outward rolling of the eyelid, usually lower lid, and may need surgical correction.

Hypertrophy of the Nictitans Gland
"Cherry eye" is the increase in size of the gland resulting in eversion of the third eyelid and is usually bilateral. Onset frequently occurs during stressful periods such as teething.

NEUROMUSCULAR SYSTEM

Epilepsy
Epilepsy is a disorder in which the electrical brain activity "short circuits," resulting in a seizure. Numerous breeds and mixed breeds are subject to idiopathic epilepsy (no explainable reason). Seizures usually begin between six months and five years of age. Don't panic. Your primary concern should be to keep your dog from hurting himself by falling down the stairs or falling off furniture and/or banging his head. Dogs don't swallow their tongues. If the seizure lasts longer than ten minutes, you should contact your veterinarian. Seizures can be caused by many conditions, such as poisoning and birth injuries, brain infections, trauma or tumors, liver disease, distemper, and low blood sugar or calcium. There are all types of seizures from generalized (the dog will be shaking and paddling/kicking his feet) to standing and staring out in space, etc.

UROGENITAL

Cryptorchidism
This is a condition in which either one or both of the testes fail to descend into the scrotum. There should not be a problem if the dog is neutered early, before two to three years of age. Otherwise, the undescended testicle could turn cancerous.

PET OWNERS & BLOOD PRESSURE

Over the past few years, several scientific studies have documented many health benefits of having pets in our lives. At the State University of New York at Buffalo, for example, Dr. Karen Allen and her colleagues have focused on how physical reactions to psychological stress are influenced by the presence of pets. One such study compared the effect of pets with that of a person's close friend and reported pets to be dramatically better than friends at providing unconditional support. Blood pressure was monitored throughout the study, and, on average, the blood pressure of people under stress who were *with* their pets was 112/75, as compared to 140/95 when they were with the self-selected friends. Heart rate differences were also significantly lower when participants were with their pets. A follow-up study included married couples and looked at the stress-reducing effect of pets versus *spouses*, and found, once again, that pets were dramatically more successful than other people in reducing cardiovascular reactions to stress. An interesting discovery made in this study was that when the spouse and pet were *both* present, heart rate and blood pressure came down dramatically.

Other work by the same researchers has looked at the role of pets in moderating age-related increases in blood pressure. In a study that followed 100 women (half in their 20s and half in their 70s) over six months, it was found that elderly women with few social contacts and *no* pets had blood pressures that were significantly higher (averages of 145/95 compared to 120/80) than elderly women with their beloved pets but few *human* contacts. In other words, elderly women with pets, but no friends, had blood pressures that closely reflected the blood pressures of young women.

This series of studies demonstrates that pets can play an important role in how we handle everyday stress, and shows that biological aging cannot be fully understood without a consideration of the social factors in our lives.

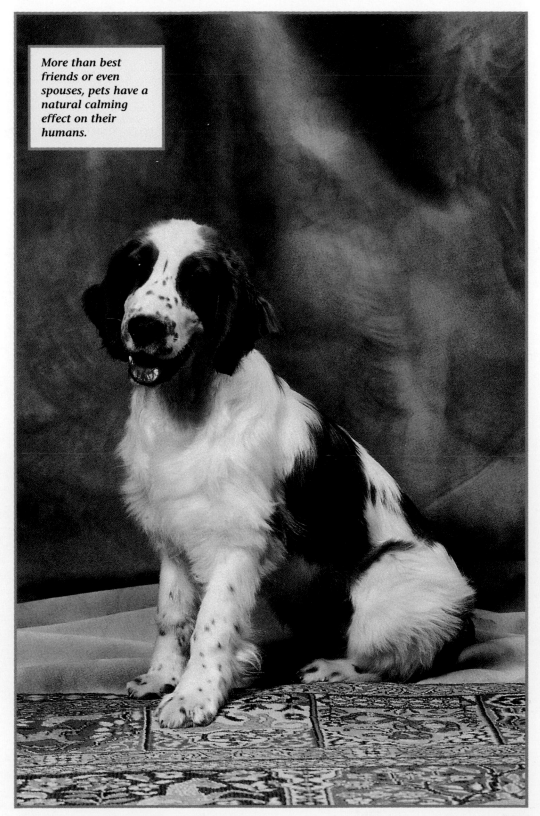

More than best friends or even spouses, pets have a natural calming effect on their humans.

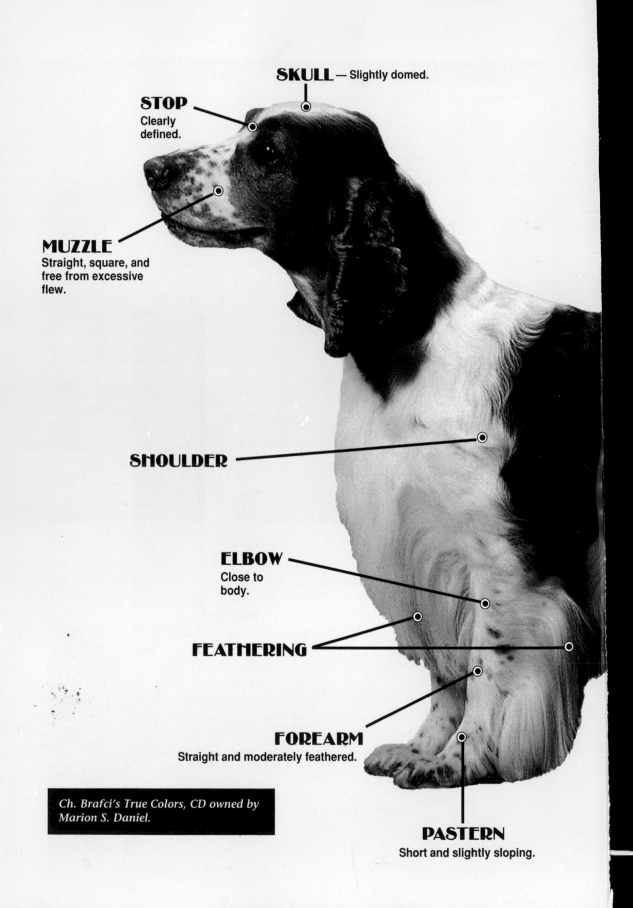

SKULL — Slightly domed.

STOP
Clearly
defined.

MUZZLE
Straight, square, and
free from excessive
flew.

SHOULDER

ELBOW
Close to
body.

FEATHERING

FOREARM
Straight and moderately feathered.

*Ch. Brafci's True Colors, CD owned by
Marion S. Daniel.*

PASTERN
Short and slightly sloping.